READINGS IN MODERN TELANGANA HISTORY

READINGS IN MODERN TELANGANA HISTORY

(Volume II)

Editor
Surepalli Venkataratnam

RESEARCH INDIA PRESS
New Delhi (INDIA)

ISBN : 978-93-5171-106-3

Price : ₹ 1850/-

First Edition: 2021

Published by :
RESEARCH INDIA PRESS
E-6/34, Sangam Vihar
New Delhi-110062
Phone: 011-26047013, (M) 9818085794
E-mail: researchindiapress@gmail.com

Type Setting by
G. R. Sharma

Contents

Acknowledgements

I am very glad to publish this book. It is a genuine pleasure to Express my sense of thankfulness to prof. K. Arjun Rao, Head, Dept. of History Arts & Social Sciences, College Osmania University, Hyderabad, Dr. B. Lavanya, Chairman, BOS, OU, Dr. G. Anjaiah, Dr. Indira, Dr. P. Ramesh, Dr. P. Aruna, Prof. A. Satyanarayana (Rtd.), Prof. G. Sudarshan Reddy (Rtd.), Prof. P. Prasangi (Rtd), Prof. G. Venkat Rajam, (Rtd.) Prof. I. Laxmi, (Rtd.) Prof. K. Ramakrishna (Rtd), Prof. R. Varalaxmi, (Rtd.), Dr. S. Anjaiah (Rtd) for their valuable suggestions and guidance to complete this book.

My sincere thanks to Dr. Pidamarthi Ravi, (Ex. Chairman, SC Corporation, T.S), Mallaiah. Battu, (Secretary MTJPBWRS, TS.). My special thanks to Dr. Moses, Director of Emily Educational Academy, Hyderabad and Dr. Konda Nageswar Rao (Joint Director, OUCIP), I am also thankful to my friends Dr. Kommu Kiran, Dr. Somapangu Ramesh, Dr. T. Venkateshwar Rao, Dr. Vempati Bhaskar for their constant support to complete this book.

I am eternally thankful to my parents Late Surepalli Chandraiah and Bhudevamma, my wife Prathibha Bashini, my daughters Thanvi & Sevitha, and also my family members who always encouraged me in completing this book.

(S. Venkata Ratnam)

Preface

This work was undertaken with great enthusiasm. This book is devoted band and obtained valuable information on different aspects on Telangana. Everyone has given their efforts to highlight their area.

Dr. G. Dayakar in his work "The role of plamer and company in Hyderabad state mentioned about the crucial role of palmer and company and provides loan facility and collected huge amount from the Hyderabad state.

Dr. P. Ramesh in his work "The popular temple culture and Jatharas in Jangaon region" gave detailed information about temple cultures and local deities in Janagoan region.

Dr. Surarapu Bixsham, in his work "Bansi raja's role in court, Darbars and public ceremonies during the reign of Nizam VI" mentioned about the Bansiraja's role in Hyderabad state particularly in Nizam VI reign, he highlighted the festivals and all the ceremonies in VI Nizam time. s

Dr. Akulapally Kumaraswamy in his work "Dalit Organisation in erstwhile Hyderabad state, he described the Jagan Mitra Mandali, and the Suneetha Bala Samajam Arundhatiya Mahasaba etc., Dalit organizations in Hyderabad state.

Dr. Surepalli Venkatratnam in his work "Art and Architecture under Asaf Jahis mentioned about the architectural designs. Falaknuma Palace, Salarjung palace, Purana Haveli Palaces in Hyderabad.

Dr. P. Muthyam in his work political parties and profile of the political leadership among the Toddy Tappers in Andhra Pradesh" mentioned about the role of Toddy Tappers in different political parties in Andhra Pradesh.

I. Potanna, in his work Biography of Baddam Yellareddy, he wrote about career of Baddam Yellareddy, he was a communist leader and also crucial role in Andhra Mahasabha and Telangana Peasants armed struggle.

Nagajanu Surepally, in his work "A Dalit prospective on Kakka novel" gave detailed information about Socio-political cultural and religious life history of dalits.

E. Somla Naik in his work "Scheduled Tribes Education development in Khammam district" describes about education development among the tribals and he covered the Enrolment dropout rate, welfare hostels and Educational institutions for the tribal students in Khammam district.

Marupu Venkatesham / Nagajanu Surepally in their work "Art and culture in Telangana" Mentioned about Telangana different festivals. Folk Jatharas and Art and Artist in Telangana region etc. should be covered.

Somapangu Muthyalaiah in his work "Festivals in Telangana, he describes about different festivals like Dasara, Deepavali, Bonalu festivals etc. have been covered.

Jella Aruna in her work "Mutiny of 1857 in Hyderabad" she wrote about 1857 revolt impact on Hyderabad state.

Nagamma Surepally in her work "Telangana Jatharalu a historical study on Peddagattu and Komuravelli Jathara, She wrote about Jatharas in Telangana and also covered Folk Jatharas and Devotees, dressing of peoples at Jatharas in Telangana.

Nemmadi Saidulu in his work "Cultural perspective on Telangana movement" mentioned about cultural changes. Telangana songs and Dhoom Dham programs during the

Telangana movement have been highlighted. Surepally Uppalaiah in his work "Role of Dalits in Hyderabad he wrote about the famous dalit leaders like Bhagyareddy Varma, B.S. Venkat Rao etc. also covered the dalit organizations in Hyderabad state.

—Editor

List of Contributors

1. Dr. G. Dayakar, Asst. Professor, Dept. of History, Dr. B.R. Ambedkar Open University, Hyderabad.
2. Dr. P. Ramesh, Asst. Professor, Dept. of History, Nizam College, Osmania University, Hyderabad.
3. Dr. Surarapu Bixsham, Associate Professor of Political Science, G.D.C., Chanchalguda, Hyderabad.
4. Dr. Akulapally Kumaraswamy, Dept. of History and Tourism management, Kakatiya University, Warangal.
5. Dr. Surepalli Venkataratnam, Asst. Professor (P), Dept. of History, Nizam College, Osmania University, Hyderabad.
6. Dr. P. Muthyam, Lecturer in History, S.V.S. Govt Degree College, Vidyanagar, Hyderabad.
7. I. Potanna, Ph.D. Research Scholar, Dept. of History, Osmania University.
8. Nagajanu Surepally, Ph.D. Research Scholar, Telugu University, Hyderabad.
9. E. Somla Naik, Ph.D. Research Scholar, P.S. Telugu University, Srisailam.
10. Marupu Venkatesham, Head, Dept. of Sculpture and painting, P.S. Telugu University, Hyderabad.

    Nagajanu Surepally, Ph.D. Research Scholar, P.S. Telugu University, Hyderabad.

11. Somapangu Muthyalaiah, Ph.D. Research Scholar, Dept. of Library Science, Osmania University, Hyderabad.
12. Jella Aruna, Research Scholar, Dept. of History, Osmania University, Hyderabad.
13. Nagamma Surepally, M.Com. (O.U), MPA, Folk Arts (PSTU), Hyderabad.
14. Nemmadi Saidulu, M.A. (Telugu Studies, T.U.), M.A. (Philosophy, O,U), B.Ed.
15. Surepally Uppalaiah, P.S. Telugu University, Hyderabad.

CHAPTER – 1

The Role of Palmer and Company in Hyderabad State-A Study

G. DAYAKAR

The Palmer and Company banking firm was new to Hyderabad but drew upon the existing community of Gujarati bankers in the city. William Palmer, Eurasian son of General William Palmer by his second wife, Faisunnissa Begum from the ruling family of the Nawab of Oudh, came to Hyderabad in 1799 and he became an officer in the Nizam's military forces[1]. He was born in Lucknow and educated in England; William Palmer commanded cavalry forces for the Nizam, winning significant victories in the rich but embattled region of Berar. In 1812 he left his position as Brigadier General in the Nizam's Bodyguard to establish a mercantile house.

Establishment of the Company

In 1810, the firm identified as the 'Old Concern', was located inside the Residency compound, later it moved to Palmer's residence just outside the Residency gates in 1814. The Firm carried on various transactions in the Nizam's territories; but it drew the attention of the British Government, for the first time when it applied, on the 30th March, 1814, to the Governor-General for permission to open a banking agency at Hyderabad, and also to exploit the timber forests on the banks of the Godavari for building ships. The application was duly forwarded by the Resident at Hyderabad, Mr. Henry Russell and taken permission from the Governor–General[2]. The Governor-General and his council finding no legitimate grounds for objection, informed the Resident to allow the House to open a banking house in Hyderabad State.

Palmer and Company's first sizeable loan to the Nizam was to pay the salaries of the Nizam's reformed troops, the Hyderabad Contingent, stationed in Berar where Palmer had served. This was termed the 'Aurangabad Arrangement' of 1818. The firm continued to advance loans to Raja Chandu Lal, attracting attention and authority from some members of the Court of Directors. A battle ensued in 1819 over the financial records of the firm, in effect the state records: Chandu Lal did not keep separate state records but endorsed those of the bankers providing funds. A hostile member of the Court of Directors in Calcutta, John Stuart, demanded the records, citing the Company's responsibility to interfere with the Nizam's internal administration given the reigning Nizams' imbecility and perverseness'. Hastings argued that existing treaties preserved the Nizam's autonomy in internal affairs, but meanwhile Palmer through the Resident Russell had turned over records of the Aurangabad Arrangement[3].

It had partners who benefited from the firm's profits and were jointly liable for its losses. It also had constituents, investors who placed money at the firm's disposal in return for a fixed annual interest rate of 12 percent (the maximum permitted to British subjects in British India – many of the constituents were British). The firm expanded rapidly, dealing in *hundis* (bills of exchange, 'native bills'), Company Bills (the Residency purchased Hyderabad *Halli Sicca* rupees used at Company treasuries), and *tankhas* or *peshkush* (charges on the revenues of specified districts). By 1812 it was offering personal loans to the Diwan Munirul-Muk and shortly thereafter government loans to Raja Chandu Lal, the latter being rapid by *tankhas* drawn on designated revenue districts[4]. The firm first attempted mercantile enterprises but was increasingly drawn into loaning money to the Hyderabad Government.

Members of the Company

The Palmer Company consisted of a few personas who joined and operated the company in connection to banking activities in the State. The prominent were, viz., William Palmer, Hasting Palmer, William Currie, the Residency Surgeon, Bankati Das, a Hindu millionaire, and Samuel Russell a friend of the Resident Russell, to whom the latter had entrusted his money to invest profitably among the members[5].

Palmer's Gujarati partner, Benkati Das, was an already established persona in Hyderabad – as a *sahukar* or banker. The family was said to be originally from Ahmadabad in Gujarat, moving to Aurangabad and then Hyderabad; it was one among some eight or nine leading Gujarati families in Hyderabad (they had marital connections in Varanasi, Burhanpur, and other places). Benkati Das was forced from the Aurangabad branch of the firm when it was looted and his father Jagmohan Das died (in the 1790s). He and an older brother moved to Hyderabad's Karwan, the locality dominated by bankers. Moreover, – there are several oral versions of his history – both of them are found to have been associated with the East India Company in Calcutta/Benares[6]. One version is that he went on to Calcutta and supplied goods to Europeans. When a mutiny took place in the late eighteenth century. Benkati Das helped some Europeans to escape by ship and gave them provisions.

He then went to Varanasi where he married Gangabai and brought her to Hyderabad in about 1800. In Hyderabad, he started with nothing, but the mother of the British political agent, Sir William Rumbold, identified him as the man who had saved her life in Calcutta and renewed their acquaintance. It may be noted that it is Benkati Das's descendants who represented this famous firm in Hyderabad during that particular period[7]. His descendants preserved not only an original partnership agreement with Benkati Das's signature in Gujarat script but William Palmer's silver sugar bowl and creamer, with Palmer's name and the date 1817. The sugar bowl and creamer are kept in the family's puja room.

Samuel Russell invested his friend's money in the Palmer and Co. Thus the Resident Russell was an interested party, when he forwarded the application of Palmer & Co., though, we find him glibly avowing before the Court of Directors, while speaking in his own defense, that he was ignorant of the fact that his money was invested by his friend Samuel Russell in Palmer & Co. The actual membership of the House of Palmer & Co., consisted of not only the above mentioned persons, but it included the Resident Russell himself, his brother Henry Russell, the Engineer Sotheby, the Assistant Resident, and George Lamb. An important member in the Company was Sir William Rumbold[8]. The popular belief among the people was that Rumbold was the son-in-law of the Governor General. Russell, who was hitherto the Patron of the firm, now began to take an active interest to gain the firm's and Sir William's goodwill.

Palmer and Company of Hyderabad

Opening of the commercial House at Hyderabad marks the beginning of the economic exploitation of the State. The patronage extended by the Resident sheltered it from all danger. Its offices were located within the precincts of the Residency building. Mr. Russell used his influence to procure for the firm, customers and funds from private sources. The firm used to borrow money at 12 percent and lend it at 25 percent. Its prospects brightened from day to day. Finding it growing in prosperity, rapidly many a European Servant of the East India Company hastened to invest his money in the firm[9]. The interest evinced by the Resident in the firm, and the very fact that the firm itself was located within the Residency buildings influenced the nobles of Hyderabad including the Minister to covet deeply.

On June 27, 1816, the firm applied to the Supreme Government to allow them to lend money to the Nizam's Government, and thus alleviate the distress of the State; while forwarding this application they also took the precaution of asking in advance, exemption from the Parliamentary Act that prohibited British subjects from advancing money to Native prices. The opinion of the Advocate-General was consulted on this point, and he gave his opinion keeping the British Territories in view. The Governor-General was anxious that the British operation against the Marathas which were being carried on at this time must be successfully carried out at any cost. Hence the necessary permission to the firm to advance money to the Nizams Government was granted.

The firm after obtaining the permission, agreed to give an advance of two lakh rupees per month, in lieu of the Nizam's Government assigning the revenues of certain districts in Berar. The districts assigned to the Palmer & Co. yielded 30 lakhs annually i.e., six lakhs – more than what the Palmers gave to the Nizam. The Palmers explained that the extra six lakhs were essential to cover any contingency that might arise "such as defects in revenues, to cover interests and to give facility to the establishment to make the required monthly payments". Thus, the actual interest levied by the firm on the loans it advanced to the Nizam's Government amounted to 25 percent. The firm in order to facilitate regular payment to the troops opened a branch at Aurangabad also. It can be said without any hesitations that from this time the "virtual plunder of the Nizam began"[10].

Rajah Chandu Lal was a person of the British Government. He was the agency through which the British hoped to mould the Hyderabad administration to their own advantage. We find Lord Hastings writing to Metcalfe "I feared that, in your dissatisfaction at not finding in Chundu Lal so perfect an instrument as you wished, you had over looked the deep engagement of the Government to uphold him"[11].

This was not the only ruse adopted by Chandulal to gain the support of the all-powerful British. In order to be in the good books of the Residency officials, he gave clandestine allowances to them. The Residency itself was "a shameful monument of rapacity" built and furnished by the poverty-stricken state, whose maintenance and repairs amounted to Rs. 2,000 a month and was secretly borne by the minister[12]. Meanwhile, the firm, feeling that it would be safer to obtain the Supreme Government's guarantee for their transactions, instigated Chandulal, to obtain sanction from the Supreme Government for taking a fresh loan of 60,00,000 Rupees from the Palmers.

Chandulal applied in 1819 to the supreme Government to allow him to borrow 60 lakhs from the Palmers so that he might clear "certain debts; advance tacavi loans to cultivators." He also showed that he would improve the administration by curtailing unnecessary expenditure to the extent of 25 lakhs of rupees annually[13].

Charles Metcalfe Efforts

Lord Metcalfe succeeded Russell as Resident at Hyderabad in December 1820. Metcalfe on his arrival found the finances of the State at the lowest ebb. He also saw that the people were flying en masse to Nagpur across the Wardha border.

Releasing the urgent necessity of reorganizing the State finances, Metcalfe asked Chandulal, to that of the Minster's disgust, to furnish him with a statement showing the income and expenditure of the State. On a careful scrutiny of the accounts submitted by Chandulal, Metcalfe found that many of the evils that prevailed in the State could be traced to the iron grip in which the Palmer & Co. held the country. He realized, that if he were to give relief to the oppressed peasantry, the first thing he should do was to rescue the country from the clutches of the Palmers[14]. Hence, Metcalfe suggested to the Supreme Government that it should raise a loan at Calcutta at the rate of 6 percent interest for the Nizam under British guarantee, so that the Nizams Government could pay off its debts to the Palmer & Co.

Hastings, at once hastened to the help of the Palmers. He not only turned down Metcalfe's proposal for raising a loan at Calcutta, but even sounded a note of warning to Metcalfe by writing "Any ill-will on your part towards the House of William Palmer & Co. must necessarily be an idle imagination".

Taking advantage of this, the Palmer & Co. started working against Metcalfe through Maharajah Chandulal, who, seeing that the Governor-General's sympathies were with the firm, and believing that the firm's support was essential for his remaining in office, duly sent reports against Metcalfe. Due to these machinations of the Palmer & Co. the Governor-General was highly incensed against the Resident and even talked of recalling him[15].

Metcalfe protested against the unconstitutional methods of the Governor-General in receiving reports against the Resident through the channels of a private firm. On Metcalfe charging Chandulal of having worked against him the latter abjectly apologized to Metcalfe and told him that he was coerced by the Palmers to do so, on the threat that they would require him to pay five lakhs if he did not act in their interest.

Metcalfe wrung out more particulars from Chadulal concerning the debts to the Palmer & Co., and by July 1822 he came to know that the total debt to the Company amounted to 83 ½ lakhs, while the State's other debts to the native bankers amounted to another 17 lakhs. He also made the startling discovery that most of the Residency officials including Russell, the former Resident, and his assistant Sotheby were secret partners in the firm, and had derived immense profits[16].

The Governor-General was so much taken in by the guile of the Palmers that he took a long time to see the truth. At this juncture, Lord Hastings left India in the beginning of the year 1823, and he was succeeded by Adams, the senior most members in the Council. Adams and his Council cut down the debt to 80 lakhs and paid off the Palmers from the British President's treasury. Ultimately, Adams succeeded in making the Governor-General see the real state of affairs, and he at last agreed to guarantee a loan to the Nizams Government on the security of the *Peshkash* of the *Circars* for twelve years.

Finally, when the claim of the firm reached Rs. 1 crore, Lord Hastings insisted on its liquidation. The Nizam signed a deed relinquishing in perpetuity his claim to Rs. 7 lakhs payable annually by the Company as quit-tent or tribute *(peshkush)* for the Northern Circars. When Governor-General Hastings received this need from Chandu Lal, he remitted Rs. 1 crore to Hyderabad to settle the claims of Palmer and Company.

However, the Governor-General's actions were censured and promoted an enquiry in England. In 1824 the firm went bankrupt[17].

Palmer and Company's bankruptcy, in turn, set in motion a disastrous financial situation for Hyderabad state. The financial arrangements resorted to after the Palmer bankruptcy in 1824 failed to ameliorate the situation. Other leading bankers, first the Marwari Puran Mal and then the Parsi Pestonji, followed Palmer and Company in supplying loans to pay the Hyderabad Contingent in Berar but the payments fell behind. By the 1840, the need to pay the Contingent had made the East India Company itself a creditor of the Nizam, as the Court of Directors member John Stuart had advocated in the 1820s: the British Resident tool over payment of the Contingent in about 1845. By 1850 the situation was drastic. The state's growing debt to the Company was used by the Residents for political bargaining, and in 1853 the Nizam was forced to cede the rich province of Berar to the British[18]. Had Hyderabad state not held for the British during the Mutiny of 1857, undoubtedly further cessions of its territory would have been sought.

Role of Others in the Company

Palmer and Company was indisputably one of the major banking firms upon which the Nizams Government relied in the early nineteenth century, and it fits easily into the history of banking firms in Hyderabad as quite unexceptional in its functions. Was it exceptional because of its Gujarati Partner, because of the combination of Eurasian and Indian partners? Palmer and Company was not the only banking firm linking Europeans or Eurasians with Gujarati and other indigenous bankers in the early and mid-nineteenth century. The Englishman Henry Dighton and Benkati Das's sister's son Kishen Das were partners for a brief period and Kishen Das's brother Hari Das was for some time in charge of Palmer's collection of revenues for the Hyderabad government. Palmer repeatedly joined with other *sahukars* in Hyderabad in various endeavors. In 1814, he and other *sahukars* together purchased a large rough diamond in the Hyderabad marker, and in 1817, he was asked by the Resident Henry Russell to mediate a dispute between Chandu Lal and a representative in Hyderabad of a Banaras banking firm. Subsequently, other Europeans were involved in the banking firms in India. William Rumbold corresponded in 1815 with 'the head of the most distinguished Portuguese business house in Madras', and in the 1840s, the south Indian banker Ramaswamy started banking in the Secunderabad Cantonment with a French partner. But it was the British whose rising power led them to 'redefine' laws and treaties and interfere in Hyderabad's internal politics[19]. Henry Dighton twice tried to put together a coalition of local *sahukars* to save the Nizam from the impending cession of Berar to the British, in 1847 and 1851. The Resident blocked these efforts, as directed by Governor-General Dalhousie, who viewed Dighton's employment by the Nizam as violating the Treaty of 1798 and who invoked the Act of Parliament forbidding British subjects to lend money to native prices[20]. The then - Resident Hastings Fraser observed that Dalhousie's consent to this local Hyderabad Syndicate loan was probably not necessary, but he followed directions.

Facilities to the Palmer Family

Palmer had good relations with his own partners and other Hyderabad banking firms. Immediately after the 1824 bankruptcy, the firm's trustees expressed their continuing confidence on William Palmer by voting him and his brother

Hastings a monthly allowance of Rs. 500, from the Resident Metcalfe. After 1824, indeed, even the English constituents of the bank who lost heavily lobbied in support of Palmer. Some 500 Europeans, mostly Britishers in government service, were listed as constituents, but there were also local Indian *sahukar* creditors. Over-extending his own bank to make the sixty-Lakh Loan, Palmer had borrowed money from other *sahukars* at very high rates, and these local *sahukars* whom Palmer reimbursed first at the time of his bankruptcy. Palmer and Rumbold tried hard to pay back their creditors, in 1832 enlisting other Hyderabad *sahukars* to buy out the interests of the bank's original creditors at a rate of about 20 per cent of the outstanding balances. After Rumbold's death in 1833, Palmer continued to try to recover the amounts owed to his firm, submitting claims for arbitration to a special court established by Chandu Lal, to *panchayats* or councils of bankers, and to successive Residents and Governor-General[21]. Gradually most of the individual debts to the firm were settled, including that of the *Diwan,* Munir ul-Mulk, whose heirs reached an agreement with Palmer in 1832 and whose debt was finally settled by the Nizam himself in 1836. In 1848, the official Persian court diary recorded the Nizam receiving *nazars* from 'Seth Pestonji and Mr. Palmer's as he journeyed from Asafnagar to Suroornagar (city suburbs). The leading banking firm that succeeded Palmer's, that of the Marwari Puran Mal, employed Palmer as a *vakil* between 1844-50, including service in 1849 to Puran Mal's son, Prem Sukh Das, in a dispute with the banker Ramaswamy. Much later, in 1867, the Resident Richard Temple noted that an important banker, Bhagwan Das (a descendant of Benkati Das's nephew, Kishen Das), was associated with the Palmers & Co. – read and corresponded with many newspapers and served as a political intermediary in Hyderabad[22].

Leading state officials including the Nizam continued to support William Palmer financially after Raja Chandu Lal was obliged by the East India Company to remove him from the state's payroll. Chandu Lal placed William Palmer on his own payroll, and in 1830 the then Resident, Josiah Stewart, found that Chandu Lal was paying Palmer Rs. 30,000 annually, a practice that Peter Wood found continuing pretty regularly until Palmer's death in 1867. When this pension was occasionally discontinued, Chandu Lal seems to have granted revenue from certain districts to Palmer instead (through a 'dependent', Mohammed Nawaz Khan). Immediately after the successful blackening of the firm's name by the lengthy British investigation instigated by Metcalfe and the firm's bankruptcy in 1824, the Nizam rewarded Palmer for opposing a plan for internal administration of the state by British officers by sending two of William Palmer's sons to school in England. The legitimate heirs of Palmer were William, Edward and Emma Palmer, who were alive in London in 1934 – and had also taken gifts from the Nizam Government[23].

The individuals most closely associated with Palmer and Company – European, Eurasian and Indian, continued to wield political power in the state despite Metcalfe's successful prosecution of the firm and the destruction of its official relationship with the Hyderabad government. The Palmers' reputation undoubtedly rested on their local services and reputation, not British support for the firm. The Palmers and others associated with this 'scandalous' firm continued to serve as government officials and political consultants in Hyderabad, arousing British disapproval upon occasion. William Palmer served the young Diwan Salar Jung I (1853-83) as an intermediary with the Paigah noble family. The Paigah family was a powerful, longstanding Sunni noble family, and Salar Jung needed its support in his early years as Diwan[24]. Palmer wrote eloquently in his own defense at length and persuasively in an undated letter to the Resident J.S. Fraser (1838-53). The Nizam himself was Palmer's patron and protector until his death in 1867.

Knowing the Governor-General predilection towards the Palmers, he assiduously cultivated their friendship. He gave regular pensions to the members of the Palmer family from the State treasury. These pensions amounted to nearly Rs.80,000 per month.

The Palmer family did not survive in Hyderabad, although members are buried in Hyderabad and Secunderabad. William Palmer lived as a Muslim, and of his seven children, five were said to be illegitimate. His third and last wife, Hester, the widow of Dr. Desmoneux, was English and they had no children. Palmer erected a tomb for his widowed mother, Bibi Daiz Baksh Faizunnaissa Begum, who lived with him after General William Palmer's death in 1816 until her death in 1828. Her tomb and a small mosque are at Troop Bazaar Hyderabad, surrounded by the graves of three waiting women (or possibly of Palmer's Muslim wives). Palmer's nephew (son of his brother Hastings), Edward Palmer, was a doctor and medical advisor to the Minister's family in 1840. James Edward Palmer, Palmer's son and father of the Edward who went to London, was known as the Blind Major of Secunderabad; he died in 1865 and was buried in Secunderabad. The grave monument of one of the last Palmers in Hyderabad, Thomas, was created in 1904 by Maharajah Kishen Pershad, Prime Minister of Hyderabad and great grandson of Raja Chandu Lal[25]. Palmer's daughter Lucy Fallon (married to Captain William Fallon of the Nizams Army) was alive in 1916 in Saifabad, and in the mid-twentieth century, Palmer's unmarried granddaughter Mobel was also getting a pension of Rs. 100 from the Nizam.

Conclusion

The palmer and Company played an important role in the State. The firm provides loan facility and collected huge amount from the Hyderabad State. The noble of Hyderabad directly and indirectly were the members of the firm and exploited not just money but also various resources of the State. After the death of the Palmer, the members of the family got pensions from the Nizam government. Nizam also sent Palmer sons to England for their education. The company borrowed money from the local bankers with 12 percent of interest and it was offered in the form loans at an interest rate of 25 percent to the Government of Hyderabad. They acquired a double-amount from the government in the form of interest. The resident Charles Metcalfe understood the intention of the firm and he convinced the Governor–General, obtained a loan from the British Government with 6 percent interest, and cleared the dues of the Palmer Company. It is one of the best examples, that portrays how the Palmer and Company exploited the Nizams wealth with the support of the nobles.

NOTES

1. *The Freedom Struggle in Hyderabad* (1800-1857). *Vol. - I*, The Hyderabad State Committee, Hyderabad, 1992. p.73.
2. Raghunadha Rao, P. *History of Modern Andhra Pradesh.* New Delhi: Sterling Publishers Private Limited, 1988. p.41.
3. Sarojini Regani: *Nizam - British Relations 1724-1857*, Booklovers Private Limited, Hyderabad, 1963, p.225.
4. Proceeding connected with the Writ of Mandamus issued by His Majesty's Court of Kings Bench, against the Court of Directors of the East India Company, *Affairs of Messrs William Palmer and Co,* London, 1833, p.47.
5. Sarojini Regani: *Nizam-British Relations 1724-1857*, Op-Cit, p. 221.

6. Karen Leonard: *Hyderabad and Hyderabadis*, Manohar Publishers & Distributors, New Delhi, 2014,P.207.
7. Paton McAuliffe, R: *The Nizam, the Origin and Future of the Hyderabad State*, Cambridge University Press, London, 1904, P.42.
8. Sri William Rumbold had accompanied the Governor-General Lord Hastings to India in 1813. Lord Hastings was greatly interested in Sir Rumbold for he had married a ward of Lord Hastings towards whom Lord Hastings evinced great affection. This deep affection of Lord Hastings made him blind to the defects in the character of the man his ward had married.
9. *The Memorial of William Palmer of Hyderabad*, 12th May, 1824, The Right Honourable Lord Amherst, Papers, P.P3-4.
10. Sarojini Regani: *Nizam-British Relations 1724-1857*, Op-Cit, P.225.
11. Jhon William Kaye: *The Life and Correspondence of Charles, Lord Metcalfe*, Vol-II, Richard Bentley, London, MDCCCLIV, PP.85-87.
12. *The Freedom Struggle in Hyderabad, (1800-1857),* Vol-I, P. 78.
13. Proceeding connected with the Writ of Mandamus issued by His Majesty's Court of Kings Bench, against the Court of Directors of the East India Company, *Affairs of Messrs William Palmer and Co*, London, 1833,161.
14 . John William Kaye: *Selections from the Papers of Lord Metcalfe*, Smith, Elders &Co, Cornhills, London, MDCCCLV, P113.
15. Karen Leonard: *Hyderabad and Hyderabadis*, Op-Cit, P. 210
16. *The Freedom Struggle in Hyderabad, (1800-1857),* Vol-I, Op-Cit, P.84.
17. Raghunadha Rao, P: *History of Modern Andhra Pradesh*, Op-Cit, P. 42.
18. Srojini Regani: *Nizam-British Relations 1724-1857*, Op-Cit, P. 298.
19. Karen Leonard: *Hyderabad and Hyderabadis*, Op-Cit, P. 215.
20. Sarojini Regani: *Nizam-British Relations, 1724-1857*, Op-Cit, P. 298.
21. Sarojini Regani: *Nizam-British Relations*, 1724-1857, Op-Cit, P. 225.

22. Karen Leonard: *Hyderabad and Hyderabadis*, Op-Cit, P. 216.
23. Sarojini Regani: *Nizam-British Relations, 1724-1857*, Op-Cit, P. 225.
24. Syed Hossain Bilgrami: *A Memoir of Sir Salar Jung,* Times of Indian Steam Press, Bombay, 1883, P. 18.
25. Grattan Geary: *Hyderabad Politics*, Bombay Gazette Press, Bombay, 1884, P. 5.

CHAPTER – 2

The Popular Temple Culture and Jatharas in Jangaon Region - A Study

P. Ramesh

The study is trying to find out the importance of Temple culture and the status of various Jatharas in Jangaon region. And the state has wanfedly encouraging to the most culture for getting the high income on the basis of ignorance and illiteracy of mass people.

According to Karl Marx "People were the creators of history, not only that they were creators of popular culture".

The temple was the most importance Vedic (Hindu) religious form of Institution[1]. From the inscriptions we gather that like..., following terms were used as synonyms for 'Temples' the Devalayamu, Degulamu, Suragaramu Thirumuttam, prasadamu, Ragudi, Meda, Devastanam, Alukumu, Stanamu, and Koyil, etc.,

The building of the temples in India was the natural corollary of the image worship which was again the result of man's desire to give definite from to the deity, the God almighty. And the building of the temple, for the idols or symbols of various deities became popular in India due to the people desire to get religious merit for themselves, and for their near and dear.

And the popular culture accumulated store of culture products such as music, literature, art, fashion, dance, film, television and radio that are consumed primarily by non-Elite groups such as the working and lower classes (as were as substantial segments of the middle class). It has attracted the intention of sociologists first in members of the Frank furt school for example, argued that popular culture is trivial, homogenized, and commercialized and dulls people's minds, making then passive and easier to control. A related argument is that because popular culture is controlled primarily by elites (through ownership of the mass media, for example) it tends to reflect their interests. The trivialization and sexual objectification of women in film for example, has been criticized by many feminists as serving the interest male viewers and male dominance[2].

And others, in particulars British societies engaged in cultural studies, argue just the opposite, that popular culture is often a vehicle for rebellion against the culture of dominant groups. From this perspective, popular culture is not a steady bland diet handed down from above in order to dull and pacify subordinate groups and reflect and promote elite interests. Instead, it is an arena full of diversity, conflict and struggle over the content of culture, and there by, the shape of social life.

The popular culture of Indus Valley Civilization comprising 'Mother Goddess' and worship of Nature got combined with later vedic gods and goddesses to form composite culture though the founders of the Aryan Civilization and the vedic had had differences their respective cultures were protected to form composite culture in the latter periods. As the centuries rolled the rituals as part these two cultures assumed the shape of religion. Further, with evolution of the human society in

India, the latter has witnessed the growth of religions like., 1. Vedic religion (or Hinduism) 2. Jainism and 3. Buddhist of the above three religions, vedic religion, influenced the Indian society, immensely and has been continuously doing so. Reason for the influence can be found in the spirituality inherent in the vedas and their practice in the daily life. Out of the sustained practice emerged different rituals, festivals, Jatharas and beliefs etc....,

The onset of Modern Government provided needed impetus to these festivals, fairs and Jatharas thus allowing them to be live. Further the government has institutionalized them in the form of patronage, construction of temples, appointment of priest's and administrators the response from the devotees has been accordingly . The inter-play of the institutionalization and the response of the devotees has strengthened the hold of region. 'Jathara' is one of the aspects of the 'organization of religion. In order to understand the Jathara and its significance it is pertinent to know the meaning of the 'Jathara'.

Definition of Jathara

People worshipping their own deities, Gods on several auspicious days of the year of the several aspects of spirituality, Jathara is one among them in Jangaon region of the Telangana state. It continuous to be so till date. 'To know is continuous significance in the Jangaon region a case of "palakurthi Jathara" is examined as an example[3].

Palakurthi Jathara

Palakurki or Palakurthi village is located 60 kms away from the old district head quarters of Warangal, and 30 kms away from the newly formatted district headquarters of Jangaon.

The famous 'Hari Hara' pilgrim centre, is situated on kshiragiri hillocks', popularly these hills are considered to be perennial source for the flow of milk from themselves. Thus the hills were named. Every year factor is held in the months of February and March in the name of the disciple of palakurthi Somanna the during the rest of the year, devotees come to offer prayers and perform rituals. 'Shiva Rathri' festival has a special significance for their temple on this day palakurthi Somanth's birth day and someshwara lakshmi Narasimha's is marriage ceremony is celebrated by the devotees with religious fevour, devotees come from the neighboring states Karnataka, Maharastra, addition to the Telangana. The state endowments ministry has been supporting in economic and administrative teams regularly as to meet the demands of the pilgrims.

The Jangaon region has been the centre state for various socio-cultural and religious fairs and festivals of temple culture. Palakurthi village being part of the region in heirs that legacy. It has assumed significance as it houses Shiva Kshetram.

Somanth is said to be lived in during 1160-1240 A.D. according to Bandaru Thammayya'. Who authored "Palakurki Somanatha Kavi"[4]. In the same work he mentions, that Somanatha has born into a 'orthodox Brahmin family. As he was born on the hills of Someshwara Swamy he has christened as Somanatha by his parents Sreeyadevi and Vishurami Devudu. Somanatha has become later, house a hold name, for example Somanna, Somakka, Somanath, Someshwar, Somla, Somani, Somhalaxmi, Somanarsaiah, Somulu, Somashekhar, and Somendar, Somabrahman etc[5].

In this way many of other Jatharas and new trends have been taken birth in this region. Some of those important Jatharas like.., below...

POPULAR TEMPLES AND JATHARAS IN JANGAON REGION

Sl. No.	*Place*	*Name of the God*	*Jathara Duration*	*Number of Visting Devotees*
1	Palakurthi	Sri Someshwara Laxmi Narasimha Swamy	Particularly (9) days, generally year long	150000
2	Valmidi	Sri Valmiki Maharshi, Sri Seetharama Chandra Swamy	10 days (Srirama Navami)	25000
3	Bammera	Sri Pothanamatya Sri Seetharamachandra Swamy	3 days	5000
4	Chinna Madura	Sri Venugopala Swamy	3 days	5000
5	Kadavendi	Sri Venkondayya Laxmi Narasimha Swamy	15 days from Holi & Ugadi	50000
6	Jeedikallu	Sri Seetharama Chandra Swamy (Veerachala hillock)	Particularly on Kartika Pournami and Srirama Navami, generally year long.	250000
7	Komaravelli	Sri Mallikharjuna Swamy	Maha Shivarathri year long	500000
8	Kodavaturu	Sri Siddeshwara Swamy	Maha Sivarathri 9 days & year long	150000
9	Bekkallu	Sri Ramalingeshwara Swamy	Mahasivarathri 9 days & year long	10000

contd. table

Sl. No.	*Place*	*Name of the God*	*Jathara Duration*	*Number of Visting Devotees*
10	Chilpuru	Sri Venkateshwara Swamy (Bugulu)	Year long	100000
11	Lingampalli	Sammakka Saralamma Tribal koya Goddesses	3 days in the month of February	50000
12	Devaruppula	Sri Uppula Mallikharjuna Swamy	5 days	5000
13	Nawabpet	Sri Kodanda Ramaswamy	7 days Srirama Navami	20000
14	Ellarayani Thorruru (Palakurthi)	Peddammadevi Goddess	5days	10000
15	Madhapuram	Sri Sevalal Maharaj of Tribal Lambadas God	3 days	20000
16	Vanaparthi	Sri Beerappaswamy	3 days	10000
17	Ammapuram	Sri Venugopalaswamy	3 days	5000
18	Govardhanagiri	Sri Venugopal swamy Sri Seetharamachandra swamy	3 days	10000
19	Ghanpur (station)	Sri Seetha Ramachandra Swamy	3 days	10000
10	Nelapogula	Hazrathsayyad Abbas shahvali	3 days	10000

A long with the above mentioned popular temples and Jatharas of the region, some other new trends were started and have been following by the people in this decade. For example, Durgamma jatharas, Bodrai installation celebrations, Sammakka-Saralamma Jatharas and lambadas Sevalal Maharaj celebrations have been celebrating by the common people in every where. These new trends are affecting the village (rural) society and its culture.

Conclusion

Historically, socio-economic, political and cultural order has been governed by religion. The religion sustains itself by reproducing and recreating itself in various spheres of social life in the society. Religion has many physical forms and practices and of its varied forms. Jathara, a festival in Telangana in for wined with the cultural life of the people.

People want a relief from day-to-day routine and mechanical life. A reason is that they having the capacity of expense i.e., betterment cost of living. Modern period and media are creating interests towards tours and entertainment. It has been increasing by the mass effect. Culture of celebrating parties on the occasions is supporting the point. Important and in-negligible angle is that benefits of the political groups and corporate or business strategies are encouraging the system towards the mass celebrations. Concept of worship is at some-what level, but celebrating is become as the important aspect. As said in the above lines, religion has been taking many forms and changing them itself from time to time to capture the mind sets of the people and to continue its domination over the people. If it is separated from the people's own interests, the culture of the people will remain as the honourable, remarkable and reasonable practice eigher it is a Jathara or a festival.

NOTES

1. Prof Soma Reddy R- History of Religious Institutions in Andhra Desha from AD-1300 -To1600, New Era Publications, Madras, 1981, pp-7-8.

2. Allam G. Johnson- The Black well Dictionary of Sociology World View publishers, New Delhi, 2000-P.268
3. Interviews with prominent persons of Palakurthi Village : (dates : 04-03-2018 to 10-03-2018)
1. B. Sadanandam Teample Executive officer
2. Devagiri Anilsharma (temple priest)
3. Panneeru Yadamma (Bangle seller)
4. Dontike Biksham (Devotee)
5. Shankaramanchi Shyam Prasad (writer)
4. Prasad, Shankaramanchi-Sahithi Vaithalikudu-Palkurthi Somanadhudu P-2
5. I bid, P-3

REFERENCES

Brake, M- The sociology of youth culture and youth subcultures- Routledge and Kegan Paul, London, 1980.

Basam, A.L- A Cultural History of India' Oxford University press, New Delhi, 1989.

Radha Krishna Sharma M- 'The Temples of Telangana' Published, Govt of A.P. Hyd. 1972.

Kodanda Ramayya T (ed)- 'Palakurki Somanatha-Anubha Saram' Published in Madras, 1957.

Ramanna, Devagiri- Sri Palakurthy Someswara Laxmi Narasimha Swamy Mahatmayam, Published in Palakurthy, 1999.

Rama Rao, M. (ed)- 'Kakatiya Sanchika', Published Archaeological Museums Department of India, Hyderabad, 1991.

Tom Bottomore- A dictionary of Marxist thought'. World View Publications, New Delhi, 2000.

CHAPTER – 3

Bansi Raja's Role in Court, Darbars, and Public Ceremonies During the Reign of Nizam VI

SURARAPU BIXSHAM

Introduction

Bansi Raja, a key personality in the Nizam's court, was most influential. He was in charge of the household affairs of the Nizam. He not only proved his competence as a head sarrishtedar, but he equally proved his influence and capacity in attending to the arrangements and organisations of Darbars, festivals, all the ceremonies connected with birth, marriages and death in the Nizam's palace. He acted as an adviser to the Nizam, and was a trustworthy companion, a mediator, a host, a poet and a literary figure. How far did this many-faceted personality succeed in performing his duties in various aspects to the expectations of the Nizam. The following pages will throw more light on his multiple roles and how his personality emerged at the Nizam's court and he achieved renown and status.

The holding of Darbars by the kings was an old custom in vogue for centuries. The Asaf Jahi rulers adopted this practice since it had been prevalent during Mughal rule. In earlier times the Darbars were usually held on issues of political importance.

But it was not so with the Nizams of Hyderabad. The Darbars were organised by the Asaf Jahi rulers on different occasions, such as the birthday ceremony of the ruling king. As Asaf Jahi rulers were symbols of Hindu-Muslim unity, the Darbars were also held on the Hindu as well as Muslim festivals, such as, Dessarah, Basant, Holi, Bakr-id, and Nauroz. These Darbars were generally known as Mughlai Darbars.

During the reign of Mir Mahbub Ali Khan Nizam –VI Darbar were usually held at Chowmahalla palace, Chowmahalla Palace was decorated and furnished in the old style with furniture, chandeliers and mirrors, and a separate place was reserved for musicians and their accompanists. The attendant would call out the arrival of the Prime Minister, Paigah nobles, Peshkar and other great noblemen and the mode of conveyance used by these personalities. All these nobles would be in traditional gorgeous Darbar dress and wearing their finest jewellery.

Bansi Raja made all arrangements on the eve of Darbars both Mughlai and English. He had the distinction for offering it and pan at the conclusion of Darbars [1]. This was an honour to his family which it held until the Independence of India.

The Mughlai and English Darbar each had their own distinct features. At the time of Mughlai Darbar, it was customary, as at other Darbars, for the harkaras to announce the arrival of the king, members of the Paigah family, Prime Minister, Peshkar and other great nobles. The seating arrangement was fixed, for the Prime Minister, Peshkar and other nobles.

The compulsory uniform for the Mughlai Darbar was dastar, jama, nima, bugloos and sword. On the arrival of the Nizarn, at the Darbar hall wearing a special costume, all present to attend the Darbar would at once rise and stand in respect to the Nizarn. After the Nizam had taken his seat on the gold embroidered royal masnad, the musicians would begin their joyous felicitations, whose seat was fixed under a satin canopy. The Nizam's retainers would take their seats behind him, in a semicircle, including Mohteshamud-Daula, son of Sultanuddin Khan Bashir-ul-Mulk with the morechal. Then all the members of the Paigah family would reach the adab-gah, or the place fixed for offering salutation, to offer adab to His Highness. Thereafter, the Prime Minister, the Peshkar and nobles would follow in order of their ranks and status to offer their adab, bowing low, seven times. The chobdars would escort these dignitaries holding their hands from the adab gah up to the Nizam to present nazr, respectfully. After presenting the nazr, they would go back to their respective seats facing the Nizam without turning their backs. Subsequently, on behalf of the government servants', purses from every department would be presented as nazrs to the Nizam. At the close of the Darbar, Bansi Raja, whose seat was fixed behind the Peshkan would present itr and pan either to the Nizam or the Prime Minister in accordance with the Mughlai or English Darbar. It was a tradition that in the English Darbars Nizam would offer itr and pan to the Resident, while in the Mughlai Darbar the Prime Minister or the Peshkar to other nobles in order of precedence and rank.

Thereafter, Tahniyat-yar-ud-Daula, vakil, between the Prime Minister and the Nizam's zanana, would exchange the pillows of the masnad, indicating the conclusion of the Mughlai Darbar. Then the nobles once again would offer their adab and depart.

On the occasion of some of the Darbars, titles, honours, and other awards were bestowed to different personalities in recognition of their meritorious services rendered to the State. Most of these titles were announced in Darbars and given when a noble returned from a battle or a mission, or when he appeared for the first time after the death of his father. Historically these titles and honours were the legacies which the Nizarns inherited from the Mughal Emperors[2]. Raja Sheoraj Dharmwant of the Malwala family, had the privilege of recommending the 'titles' to the Nizam, being head of the office of Manasib-O-Khirabar. It was customary that the Nizam would bestow jewels on the appointment of a Diwan and peshkar and to other nobles on the occasion of their marriage. The responsibility of recommending the jewels to be bestowed to the nobles rested with Bansi Raja.

The scene of the Mughlai Darbar would remain incomplete without the description of the bestowal of jewels and titles. For instance, in 1894, the Nizam enquired of Bansi Raja the procedure followed in the past for the bestowing of jewels and Robes of honour to be presented to Viqar-ul-Umara on his appointment as Diwan or Prime Minister[3].

A Darbar was organised at Khilwat and Bansi Raja, as usual, made the arrangements adhering to the Asaf Jahi traditions. Viqar-ul- Umara arrived wearing the robes of honour. On arrival at the Darbar hall, he went to the Nizam, offered his adab, seven times, bowing low. Then he respectfully presented the nazr to the Nizam. Bansi Raja handed over the jewels one by one to the Nizam, who in turn bestowed them on Viqar-ul-Umara.

The following seven pieces of jewellery were bestowed on Viqar-ul—Umara:

1. Diamond serpech with emerald pearls.
2. Diamond turrah with pearl string
3. Diamond har with emeralds
4. Pearl kanthi with diamond pendent
5. Diamond dastband
6. Diamond bhujband
7. Diamond bazuband with pearls

Details of the Robes of Honour

Seven items of the mulbus (clothes) of Afzal-ud-Daula Nizam-V were offered as Robes of Honour to Viqar-ul-Umara.

1. Dastar Sandli
2. Turrah Muqqaish
3. Jama Sandli with masala Karchobi
4. Parka with Kinari
5. Nima Sandli
6. Pyjama brocade
7. Goshpech Karchobi

Besides jewellery and Robes of Honour, the Nizam also presented him with a sword and doshala. Viqar-ul-Umara went back to his palace in amari in a procession[4]. During the same Darbar Nizam bestowed titles on many nobles some of them were[5]: Afsar Jung, Afsar-ud-Daula, Sarwar Jung, Sarwar-ul-Mulk, Raja Murli Manohar, Asaf , Nawazwant, Raja Girdhari Pershad, Mahbub Nawazwant.

Thus Darbars were not only the backbone of the Nizam's court but were also specimens of pomp and splendour. These Darbars were usually held late in the evening. Generally, the Darbar hall was

Brilliantly illuminated by beautiful crystal chandeliers; there were musicians with their musical instruments in the traditional fashion, the noise of the movements of people in the crowded hall presenting an enchanting effect upon the scene. The glamour and the pageantry of the Darbar dazzled the eyes of the spectators.

The Darbars were also organised on the occasion of the visits of Govemor-Generals and the Residents. The reception Darbars were held to welcome the incoming Residents and to bid farewell to the outgoing Residents. During these Darbars a "khareeta" or letter, addressed to the Nizam, was presented by the Residents. These were generally referred to as English Darbars, The Residents of Hyderabad were never allowed a chair in the past in such Darbars. The Resident and other British officials would sit on the carpet to the right, bare-headed and without shoes, in the presence of the Nizam till the end of Afzal-ud-Daula, Nizam-V's reign. The Resident once petitioned the Nizam that the practice of squatting on the floor at the time of Darbar was highly inconvenient to a man wearing breeches and that he should be allowed the use of chairs in the Darbar. The Nizam ordered that a pit should be dug to enable the Resident to lower his legs, and thus the question was settled[6].

After the death of Afzal-ud-Daula, the Diwan and the Paigah noble Amir-i-Kabir decided to install Mir Mahbub Ali Khan on masnad as the ruler and presented nazr without the knowledge of the Resident. When the Resident received this news, he was angry, since they had dispensed with his presence and advice; he showed his anger by becoming obstinate and insisting that chairs be provided in the Darbar, otherwise he would not take off his shoes or attend the Darbar. Sir Salar Jung and Amir-i-Kabir were forced to oblige and accede to his conditions. Thereafter, chairs were introduced in the Asaf Jahi Darbars.

Sir Richard Meade, the then Resident, once desired to visit His Highness and interview him privately at any time, according to his convenience. This was contrary to the established rule of the Darbar. Since the Nizam was a young boy the idea of meeting the Nizam alone was not liked by any of the nobles, but the request could also not be refused. Sir Salar Jung especially instructed Bansi Raja, knowing that he would handle such a delicate situation, to take suitable steps. He also posted some harkaras on the Afzal Gunj Bridge to inform the concerned nobles on the arrival of the Resident.

One day, the Resident came up to the Afzal Gunj Bridge. The harkaras, as instructed, went in all directions and informed Bansi Raja, who, according to the instructions of Sir Salar Jung, informed the concerned nobles. When the Resident reached the palace he was given a guard of honour. In the meantime Sir Salar Jung, Amir-i- Kabir, and other nobles had arrived. It was a strange emergency Darbar that thus assembled like the Mughlai Darbar, the seating arrangement for the English Darbar was also fixed. The Prime Minister, Peshkar and other nobles would sit on the left side of the Nizam and the Resident and British officials on the right.

In 1877, the Viceroy and Governor-General of India arranged a grand finale and a lavish Darbar to celebrate the assumption of the title of Kaiser-i-Hind by Queen Victoria. The ruling chiefs, Rajas,nawabs of Princely States — including H.H. the Nizam - and all the nobility, were invited to attend the Darbar. Mir Mahbub Ali Khan went to Delhi along with Sir Salar Jung, the Peshkar and a largeentourage. The itinerary of the journey including halts was prepared. Bansi Raja, along with superintendents of other departments of the Royal house, elephants, horses and carriages, were sent in advance for necessary arrangements. African Cavalry guards, Myseram regiments, or Nazm-i-Jamiat, Regular Troops, the Arabs, and the Paigah forces accompanied the royal party.

The royal camp at Delhi was finely decorated and illuminated in the old Mughlai style. Similarly, other camps were arranged for the nobles of Hyderabad according to their ranks, under the supervision of Bansi Raja. All the British officials were present at the Delhi railway station, with troops, colours and band, to receive the Nizam.

The Darbar at Delhi was organised on a vast ground. The seat of the Viceroy was arranged on a raised platform. This platform was hexagonal in shape and decorated with colours like red, blue, and gold. The length of this platform was 240 feet, with stairs in front and back having golden railings. The platform was covered with a canopy. On each corner of the canopy satin flags were hoisted bearing the symbol of the Union Jack. Guards were stationed on both sides of the raised platform to present the guard of honour. Guns were placed around the platform[7].

Opposite the Viceroy's platform a semicircular platform decorated with blue, white and gold colours was erected for the ruling princes and chiefs. This platform was 236 feet away from the platform of the Viceroy. This semicircular platform was 800 feet in length and had thirty-six divisions. Each division was thirty feet in length and twenty feet in breadth. The photographs of the royal crown were placed on the four corners of the platform. Costly carpets were laid for the ruling princes and chiefs. Chairs with colourful logos to differentiate between the princes and the chiefs were placed on the platform.

A special seating arrangement was made for the Nizam Mir Mahbub Ali Khan. His seat was arranged opposite the seat of the Viceroy Lord Lyton in the centre of the semicircular platform. On the right hand side of the Nizam, the Rajput princes and on his left the ruling chiefs of Central India and Punjab were seated.

On another Platform, seats were reserved for the 'British officials nobles and other dignitaries. Bansi Raja was provided a chair on the same platform meant for the nobles.When all the guests occupied the seats, the Viceroy arrived. All present welcomed the Viceroy with loud applause and congratulatory slogans. The aide-de-camp of the Viceroy read out the address of the Queen Victoria in English, which was subsequently translated into Urdu. In brief, the Queen additionally held the title of Empress of India or Kaiser-i-Hind. Afterthe Viceroy's address a royal salute of 101 guns was fired from behind the platform, where twenty thousand army personnel were present with artillery[8].

The first anniversary of the assumption of the title by the Queen was celebrated at the Residency of Hyderabad. Sir Richard Meade the Resident in 1878, held a Darbar at the residency. Sir Richard Meade, accompanied by Sir Salar Jung-I, Nawab Shams-ul-Umara Amir-i-Kabir entered the Darbar hall followed by a number of principal city nobleman. The Resident reviewed the achievements of 1877-78. In his address he mentioned the effects of the severe famine which had hit greater of Bombay and Madras presidencies. He expressed his appreciation of the Nizam's Government for bearing the full share of the burden and the effectual means the State had taken to meet the distress. He also complimented the regent and co-regent on the improvement in the health of the young Nizam. He earnestly hoped that his education would he eminently successful, and that it would prepare him for the high and responsible position to come. The Darbar concluded with thanks to all present for their attendance. Thereafter garlands were offered to the guests[9].

Soon after the death of Sir Salar Jung in 1883 and prior to the installation ceremony in 1884, the Nizam had to face serious problems. The interference of the then Resident and the rivalry between the nobles for the post of Diwan were the main causes. Hence, the Nizam was advised by some of his well wishers to have a dialogue with the Viceroy, Lord Ripon, regarding the confused affairs of the State.

The Nizam, along with the Peshkar and other nobles, went to Calcutta. Bansi Raja left in advance in order to make the arrangements for the Nizam's journey to various places, and his halts, before reaching Calcutta. He made all necessary arrangements at Shahabad, the first stop of the Nizam. At Gulbarga, he arranged for the preparation of muzafir for niaz at the tomb of the Muslim saint,Khwaja Banda Nawaz. Bansi Raja then reached Calcutta before the arrival of the Nizam.

The Nizam arrived at Calcutta on 22nd December 1883. The Resident was present at the Calcutta railway station to welcome the Nizam. Calcutta Station was decorated with flowers and illuminations. The personal bodyguard of the Governor-General presented a guard of honour. In the past no other ruling prince or chief had been accorded such a ceremonial reception. The British treated the Nizam with due respect and gave him a royal and red carpet reception. The Resident accompanied the Nizam up to his camp. The Nizam was accommodated at a grand and beautiful bungalow (hired at 8,000.rupees rent by Mr Wilkinson, secretary, buildings), specially decorated and arranged for the Nizam. The Asaf Jahi yellow flag, which was made at Hyderabad and taken by Barisi Raja, was hoisted in the courtyard of the building. The Raja also arranged naubat and roushan chowki to be played at the stated intervals. Bansi Raja wrote that the people of Calcutta were surprised to see the Asaf Jahi flag. None of the other visiting ruling princes had the privilege of hoisting their flag.

The Nizam, accompanied by a large entourage, called on the Governor-General, Lord Ripon. On his arrival at the palace of the Governor-General a twenty-one gun salute was presented to the Nizam. The Darbar at Calcutta had its own significance. The same evening the Governor-General paid a return visit to the Nizam along with sixteen high officials.

A canopy was erected on the balcony of the said building, where seating arrangements for the Governor-General were made. The Governor-General sat next to the Nizam. British officials on the right and the nobles of the Nizam occupied their seats on the left during the Darbar. The Governor-General expressed his happiness over the visit of the Nizam and said that a cordial relationship should be developed between the two governments. In order to strengthen their cordial relations, he declared that he would attend the Installation ceremony of Mir Mahbub Ali Khan at Hyderabad on 17th February, 1884. Subsequently, an official notification was issued. Thereafter, Bansi Raja offered silver pandan at the express wish of the Nizam. Some of the British officials offered nazr to the Nizam on the advice of the Resident of Hyderabad, Mr J.G. Cordery. Bansi Raja submitted two Silver itrdan and a pandan to the Nizam who then offered them to the Governor-General. Raja Narender presented itrdan to other British officials[10].

February 5th, 1884 will always be remembered as a red-letter day in the history of Asaf Jahi rule, because a week-long birthday celebrations, such as, Ratjaga, Jahaz, Dhamal, Niaz, Mehndi, Aliband, besides the Installation ceremony of Mir Mahbub Ali Khan Nizam VI were arranged on his reaching eighteen. The accession ceremony coincided with the birthday of the Nizam. Hence, the rejoicing all over the city was manifold. The citizens of Hyderabad had a chance to witness the Installation ceremony after many years. Therefore, efforts were made to make this ceremony a memorable event in the history of the State. People belonging to different castes and communities participated wholeheartedly wearing gorgeous clothes.

Raja Girdhari Pershad has given a detailed description about the birthday, Aliband and installation ceremonies in his Daily Diary of 1884. He wrote that special arrangements were made to illuminate the entire city, especially the Nizam's palace, Charminar, Chahar kaman, and the entire route from where the Viceroy was to pass through to Alwal. The entire route was decorated with flowers and coloured lights. It is believed that such extraordinary illuminations had not been arranged in the previous two hundred years. The occasion marked with the visit of the Governor-General and Viceroy of India, Lord Ripon, who was the first Viceroy to visit Hyderabad for the installation ceremony. Mir Mahbub Ali Khan was the first ruler whom the Viceroy himself installed on the masnad.

The Viceroy arrived at Hyderabad station on 2nd February 1884, where a grand reception awaited him. The Nizam, his Prime Minister and nobles, along with the then Resident J. G. Cordery, Military Secretary, and other British officials welcomed the Viceroy. A guard of honour and a thirty-one gun salute were presented to him. The Viceroy then went to Bolaram Residency.

On 4th February at 10 o'clock, Mir Mabub Ali Khan went to Alwal, along with his nobles and other officials. Excellent arrangements were made on the entire route from the royal palace to Alwal. On both the sides of the roads, the Nizam's State police, Regular Force and palton were deployed. When the Nizam reached Alwal, where a camp was arranged for the Viceroy, a twenty-one gun salute was given to the Nizam from the Hussain Sagar Artillery. The Nizam met the Viceroy and after some time presented him with a garland and itardan. Thereafter, the Viceroy had an hour-long meeting with the Nizam in solitude, and then the meeting concluded. At four o'clock the Viceroy paid a return visit to the royal palace and met the Nizam.

On 7th Rabi ul sani (February 5th, 1884) a Darbar was organised, for the Investiture Ceremony. Before the arrival of the Viceroy at Khilwat Mubark, a letter was sent to the Nizam by the Viceroy, through a British official, advising the Nizam to appoint Munir-ul- Mulk as Prime Minister.

The Nizam called Raja Girdhari Pershad and while mentioning about the letter of the Viceroy's, he enquired from Raja Girdhari Pershad about the procedure of the confirmation of the robes of honour "which were to be awarded to Munir-ul-Mulk on his appointment as Prime Minister. The Viceroy, Lord Ripon, arrived at Khilwat at about ten hours. The Nizam, Mir Mahbub Ali Khan, welcomed him at the entrance of the palace. Two chairs were especially kept in front of the throne (takht). The nobles of the State, dignitaries and British officials occupied their respective chairs in accordance with their rank and status. The ceremony commenced with the detail address of the Governor-General.

In his address, the Viceroy stated that, fortunately, during the period of the Nizam's minority, he had the late Sir Salar Jung-I serving as Prime Minister, who was reckoned to be among the leading administrators of India. Even after facing many difficulties and problems, Sir Salar Jung introduced many reforms, raised the income of the State and maintained peace and tranquillity. But unfortunately, God had taken him away at a time when he was needed. It was a matter of great regret that he was not present on that occasion. "Though he is not alive, his achievements exist." The Viceroy then gave the Nizam inspiring advice in his address. He stated that the Nizam had a great and arduous task, since he was the ruler of ten million people whose welfare depended on him. He had noble aims to follow and great deeds to do. Thereafter the Foreign Secretary read the Persian version of the English speech of the Viceroy. The address of the Viceroy was replied to by the Nizam.

The Viceroy then took the Nizam to the throne and, addressing him with his full titles said that on behalf of Her Majesty, the Empress of India and the Government, "You are invested with full powers of your State." There was a gun salute from the Gosha Mahal artillery and the Myseram band played a salutation. After some time, an official on behalf of the Governor-General presented the Nizam a studded bagloos and a studded sword. The Governor-General himself adorned the Nizam with bagloos and sword. Besides this, he presented the Nizam seven horses, a watch and dorbeen (telescope).

He also presented one studded watch and a sword to Munir-ul- Mulk; a tray with similar items was presented to Raja Rajayan Narendar, and one toda and sword to Amir-i-Kabir Khurshed Jah and one tray to Bashir-ud-Daula. Thereafter, the Peshkar offered itr and pandan to the British officials, and nobles, and thus concluded the Installation Ceremony.

After the conclusion of the Darbar, Girdhari Pershad, along with Shahamat Jung, went to the haveli of Manjhli Begam and the jewellery room was opened. As usual, he presented the Nizam the list of the jewels to be awarded to Munir-ul-Mulk and other nobles on the occasion of the Mughalai Darbar schedule to be held on the same day at 3.30 at Khliwat Mubarak.

At 3.30 p.m. the Nizam arrived and seated himself on the masnad. The nobles presented the Nizam, nazr on the occasion of his accession to the throne, Munir-ud-Daula was present in the Darbar wearing the Robes of Honour in accordance with custom. It was customary to award, the Prime Minister on appointment a khilat containing yek parcha (one cloth), seh parcha (three cloths), panch parcha (five cloths), or hafi parcha (seven cloths) usually, a full khilat include arms, a horse and an elephant, besides jewels. As Salar Jung ll was appointed Madar-ul-Maham, he was bestowed panch parcha khilaz jewelled sarapa which is as follows:

Sarpatti diamonds with jigah, turrah diamond, bazuband navraran. Bhujband diamonds, dastband diamonds, kanthi pearls with diamond pendent, diamond har. Later, similar jewels were bestowed on Raja Rai Rayan Raja Maharaja Narayana Pershad Narender there after some of the nobles were awarded the titles. In this Darbar, as mentioned earlier Girdhari Pershad was awarded the title of 'Raja Bahadur.

A banquet was arranged for the Governor-General at night in Aafzal Mahal. The entire route of Charminar, Khilwat Mubarak to Alwal was illuminated. The Viceroy attended the dinner, along with two hundred British officials. There are no words to describe the arrangements of the illuminations in the city. The dinner was served on a gold dinner service set. The Governor-General himself, and most of the officials, said that they had not seen such elaborate illuminations in the whole of India. They went round the palaces of the Nizam. The banquet concluded at three in the early morning hours; thus reminding the people of the pomp and gaiety of the Darbar of Akbar and Shah Jahan, the Mughal rulers.

Aliband Ceremony

The origin of Aliband, a precious ceremonial jewel, dates back to the Prophet Ali. It was an ancient ceremony. This was a prerogative that has belonged to the Nizams for nearly two centuries.

The Aliband ceremony was conducted at the Nizarn's Palabe on 6th Rabi-ul-Sani 1301 H (1884) at Khilwar Mubarak prior to the installation of Mir Mahbub Ali Khan on masnad. Bansi Raja further wrote in his Daily Diary that this ceremony was performed at midnight. The Aliband consisted of a gold star studded with diamonds and within a ring the motto is inscribed, in Arabic: "Greatness is for God alone. "One ancient sword was also brought from the Toshak khana. Raja Narender, other nobles, Raja Girdhari Pershad, Shahamat Jung, Tahniyat-yawar-ud-Daula, Muzaffer Jung and Shuja-ud-Daula were present on this occasion. Munir-ud-Daula joined later. Shah Nooruddin Qadri performed the Aliband ceremony. Tahniyat yawar-ud-Daula offered garlands to the Nizam. Raja Girdhari Pershad offered studded Sehra and Aliband. Mirasans entertained the courtiers present with melodious songs. In recognition of his services, Girdhari Pershad was awarded Kanthi marwarid (pearl string) and a serpech. The Aliband ceremony was concluded with the offering of garlands to the courtiers present.

The Nizam wore the Aliband for the second time at Ootacomand during May 1885. The Times of India, Telegraph and Deccan Herald gave much publicity to the dinner hosted by Nawab Munir-ud-Daula in honour of the institution by the Nizam of a new order called the order of the Asafia. The papers stated, that this was the revival of an old decoration or order of Aliband and the Nizam had found this order for the distinguished public services rendered by the Government officials and others.

The Nawab said that the high distinction would be conferred on those who proved themselves worthy of the honour and would have three grades. This led to many queries and much explanation from the Minister Munir-ul-Mulk by the then Resident at Hyderabad, Mr J. G. Cordery. The then Viceroy indicated that Her Majesty's pleasure would have to be taken before a consent to the institution of any order.

The mistaken reporting of the newspapers led to confusion in the mind of the British Resident at Hyderabad. According to the Residency Records under the Foreign Department, secret despatches,numbers one to fifteen of 1885, there was an exchange of correspondence between the Resident, Nawab Munir-ul-Mulk Salar Jung II and the Foreign Secretary, H. M. Durand, on "Revival of ancient order (Aliband)".

Nawab Salar Jung replied that it was not a new order at all but, on the contrary, it was an ancient one. The Nizams used to wear Aliband on the occasion of the ceremony of their accession to the masnad and Mir Mahbub Ali Khan also wore it on the evening of his installation. He further wrote that it used to be conferred by the Nizams to the nobles. He had in his possession the insignia which was conferred on his father, the late Sir Salar Jung, by the late Nasir-ud-Daula. Therefore, it was not correct to say that a new order was being created. If changing of the name of the order and the proposal to introduce three grades has led to this misunderstanding, His Highness would be most happy to abandon his intention of renaming the order, allowing it to retain its old name.

With regard to the expression 'Order', Nawab Salar Jung wrote:

> I would point out that we do not intend to apply the word in the way in which it is usually understood in a matter of this kind. The 'Order', as I hope I have made clear in my previous correspondence on the subject, was never meant to be one in the commonly received sense of the term, certainly it was far from His Highness's intention to desire to enter into competition in the bestowal of honours of this kind with the Ruler of India, and I gather from your letters that there was an impression that such was the object we had in view in re-establishing and renaming the 'Order'. On the contrary, as we understand it, the 'Order' is simply a distinction (remaining in the family upon the head of which it was conferred, as in my case) similar to the jewelled plumes and other marks of distinction, such as the Mahi-o-maratib, Morechal, Saropa, etc., which i some of the Hyderabad nobility and other subjects of His Highness are entitled to wear. It is simply because we can find no other English equivalent for it (corresponding to the Urdu word 'Nishan') that it has been called an 'Order'. I hope you will kindly make this point clear to the Government of India, as I consider it of considerable importance.

Subsequently, it was clarified that the Viceroy had no wish to interfere with His Highness's prerogative. Perhaps the paramount power wanted to make the Nizam realise his "limited sovereignty". It might have thought that being ruler of a large Native State, the Nizam should not claim his sovereignty on equal terms by instituting a new "honorary order", which the British believed it was their absolute right to do.

On the 3rd November, 1892, Lord Lansdowne, the Viceroy, visited Hyderabad. He was welcomed by the Nizam of Hyderabad on arrival at Hyderabad railway station. The Regular Troops of the Nizam's forces presented a guard of honour and a thirty-one gun salute. The Nizam and Prime Minister hosted lunches and dinners in honour of the Viceroy's visit. A water party at Miralam tank, hunting at Saroor Nagar, and sports were organised at Malkpet.

Next day, the Viceroy paid a return visit to the Nizam. Following the programme, four officials of the Nizam's government escorted the Viceroy to the Nizain's palace, along with the Resident. He was given a ceremonial reception on arrival at the palace by the Nizam and taken to the Darbar hall for an English Darbar. The Viceroy was seated on the right-hand side of the Nizam along with foreign secretary, the brigadier general commanding the Hyderabad contingent, the officer commanding the Secunderabad District, the private and military secretary of the Viceroy, the officer of the foreign department, on special duty, and His Excellency's personal military staff.

On the left-hand side of the Nizam, the Resident of Hyderabad, The Prime Minister, the Paigah nobles, the Peshkar, other nobles, high dignitaries and officials were seated in order of precedence find ranks. All invited to the English Darbar, except the British officials, had to wear breeches, a long coat, dastar, belt and sword. The Resident introduced the Prime Minister and other nobles and officials of the State to the Viceroy. Each of these dignitaries presented five ashrais to the Viceroy. Bansi Raja submitted garlands, itrdans and pandans to the Nizam, who in turn offered them to the Viceroy. The Resident and other British officials accompanying the Viceroy received the same from the Prime Minister. Thus was concluded the English Darbar. The Nizam's army stationed in a line on both sides of the palace courtyard presented a guard of honour and a thirty-one gun Salim[11].

Sitting on the chair in the Darbar, presenting it and pan probably does not sound good in the present-day context, but the analysis of the study indicates that there were three important aspects of the Darbars: the management, recommendation of titles, and other awards. The responsibility of management, the organisation of Darbars, and the proposing of robes of honour and jewels rested with Bansi Raja. Recommendation of titles rested with Raja Sheoraj Dharamwant of Malwalas.

Bansi Raja's loyalty and faithfulness towards the ruler is unquestionable. Bansi Raja had the privilege of advising the young Nizam on many occasions, since he had the experience. The responsibilities of Bansi Raja were not confined to the arrangements of Darbars. The following pages will throw more light on the multifaceted role of Bansi Raja in the management of the household affairs of the Nizam's palace. Hyderabadies should be grateful to the Asaf Jahi rulers, who brought different religions together, sowing the seeds of nationalism and integration - and thus the development of a common culture and common language, two essentials of nationalism, which came about as a result of the fusion. The people stuck together for good and evil and they were proud inheritors of a common culture, common language, and common traditions.

The Nizams, especially Mir Mahbub Ali Khan-, made no distinction between Hindus, Muslims, and people of other religions. There was no discrimination in the award of titles, jewels, robes ofhonour, and other distinctions. The post of Prime Minister was occupied by both Hindus and Muslims. Besides the hereditary post of Peshkar and appointment of Hindus to the post of Prime Minister, the most prominent were the Hindu families of Raja Rai Rayan and Raja Sheoraj Dharamwant of Malwalas, who were entrusted with the State records of Daftar-i-Diwani and Dafiar-i-Mal, which were the very foundation of the administration of the State. The Nizam Mir Mahbub Ali Khan believed that Hindus and Muslims were his two eyes. Damage to one religion he considered as damage to his own eye.

Prior to the appointment of a tutor for the heir apparent, Osman Ali Khan, he had to appear before Mir Mahbub Ali Khan for final consent. During the conversation the tutor asked Nizam-VI how, being a Muslim himself, he had entrusted the management of the bawarchi khana of the Nizam to the charge of a Hindu. Immediately, the Nizam-Vl ordered that this person should not be appointed as the tutor, since he apparently had ill-feelings towards Hindus.

It was but natural for the then Asaf Jahi ruler to entrust the entire responsibility of the management of the palace on the shoulders of a trusted man, Bansi Raja, who happened to be a Hindu. Bansi Raja looked after all the zanana and 'mardana affairs of the palace. He made arrangements for the Darbars, and for the celebration of different festivals, for marriages and religious ceremonies connected with the palace, for about fifty years. Besides this, the confidential and delicate matters connected with the palace were also entrusted to him by Mir Mahbub Ali Khan.

Bansi Raja was in charge of various departments of the Nizam's palace. He was real controller of palace affairs. Though the responsibility of the management of the Nizam's palace and the office may be considered as an ordinary assignment, it was not so. In fact, to manage the affairs of the Nizam's palace was a very delicate and formidable task. It required talent, maturity, and tact, as the person holding such responsibilities not only dealt daily with the Nizam but also with Begams and the Nobles of the State. Bansi Raja faced situations such as the occasion of the marriage of Mir Mahbub Ali Khan's sister. The Nizam was not happy with the joda and jewels sent to one of his Begams by the groom. Also, Bansi Raja was in an awkward position because of the proposed marriage of the Nizam's sisters to the sons of Salar Jung-I. On the other hand, he had to respect the wishes of the Nizam and at the same time had to deal with the begams, who.-were strict followers of Islam - a difficult task indeed for Bansi Raja to deal with them.

Bansi Raja was gentle, affable, and courteous, besides being tolerant in religious and social matters, and having great foresight. He was neither selfish nor ambitious in any sense of the word, and was free from envy and jealousy. As a result of these qualities, he could manage the entire affairs of the Nizam's palace for decades. He carried out his duties and responsibilities so successfully and unfailingly that he received warm commendation from His Highness and the nobles. All retained full confidence in him.

It was a custom of the Mughals that during the month of 'Safar', gold and silver rings were distributed among the nobles and high officials according to their status, varying from seven to eleven rings. This custom was also adopted by the Asaf Jahi rulers.

The Nizam sent a letter to Bansi Raja asking him to furnish the details of the silver and gold rings required on 'Akhiri Chahar

Shambah' the last Wednesday of the month of 'Safar' according to Hijri calendar, which is observed by Muslims with solemnity and rejoicing in memory of the recovery of the Holy Prophet from a very serious illness. The Nizam further enquired how many of these silver and gold rings were to be distributed amongst nobles" and Bansi Raja had to arrange in advance for a large number of such rings.

In the month of Rajab the konday feast is celebrated in honour of one of the Imams. Bansi Raja also arranged the konday feast at Khilwat, the Nizam's palace. Konday is an earthenware vessel. During this feast the food was served in konday or earthenware vessels. Bansi Raja arranged this feast in an open yard of the Khilwat by enclosing it with a canopy. These guests attended the said feast, on behalf of the Nizam, and were all common citizens, not the nobility.

On a raised platform the seating arrangement for the Nizam was made. Below the platform dastarkhwan, or a piece of cloth, was spread on a covered veranda, on which the dishes of food were placed. The guests would come to the dastarkbwan, and after partaking of the food they would stop aside in front of the Nizam, salute him, bowing low respectfully, and then go back to their respective seats[12].

Nauroz, New Year's Day in the Persian calendar, was celebrated by the Mughals and also by the Nizams till 1920; when Darbars were held, titles were bestowed. In accordance with the custom, Bansi Raja would arrange for the distribution of eggs on behalf of the Nizam to various dignitaries.

The distribution of fireworks on the occasion of Shab-i-barat, the fifteenth night of the month of Shaban, from the Nizam's palace, was in vogue. Bansi Raja was entrusted with the responsibility of its distribution. Similarly on Bakr-id he would arrange the distribution of camel flesh.

The distribution on such occasions was on the basis of rank and status - such as the Prime Minister, Paigah nobles, Peshkar, other nobles and those who attended the royal palace. On some occasions a general distribution was made to all the servants of the palace, and the mansabdars without any distinction, especially in the case of the distribution of mangoes.

During mango season in 1887, the Nizam ordered Bansi Raja to arrange fifty trays of mangoes for distribution at the Saifabad Palace. It was customary at the royal palace to perform niaz of different sufi saints on the occasion of a marriage, a birthday, etc. Niaz and dhamal were arranged by Bansi Raja, in consultation with the Begams. The niaz of these sufi saints was offered with different food items, such as biryani, halim, aash, muzafir, etc. Bansi Raja would fix the date for the niaz of a particular sufi saint and accordingly the niaz was offered.

Being a tolerant ruler, the Nizam-VI always respected the advice of the Brhmins. Bansi Raja made donations on behalf of the Nizam to temples, Brahmins, and religious saints, on different occasions.The grants made by the Nizam were not restricted within the State, but also outside Hyderabad. During his travels, Nizam-VI instructed Bansi Raja to perform puja, and donate generously on behalf of the Nizam's Government. During his visit to Calcutta in 1883, Mir Mahbub Ali Khan ordered Bansi Raja to donate 2,500 rupees for the feast of the Brahmins at Benares and a brocade canopy for the Kali temple at Calcutta. On certain occasions costly jewellery was offered at these and many other temples on behalf of the Nizam by Bansi Raja.

The services of the Brahmins were always well attended and looked forward to in the Nizam's palace. They were always consulted about the planetary configuration of the Nizam and that of the members of the royal family while preparing the horoscope and for celebrations of auspicious occasions. As a well-wisher of his ruler, Bansi Raja himself prepared the horoscope of the Nizam and his other family members, as he himself was an expert in astrology. On the birth of a child at the royal palace, he would prepare a horoscope. If the signs and portent were unfavourable, he would immediately act upon them and would request the Nizam for alms to counter the bad omens.

In 1893, Bansi Raja noted that the Nizam was passing through a bad period. He submitted a petition requesting the Nizam for a tuladan. The Nizam gave his consent for the tuladan, thus Mir Mahbub Ali Khan not only maintained a tolerant attitude but gave due weight and regard to the suggestion of Bansi Raja. Subsequently, the tuladan was arranged on the occasion of His Highness' birthday[13].

Bansi Raja composed a poem consisting of fifty-eight couplets in Persian on the occasion of tuladan, narrating the entire sequence of the ceremony. He wrote that the word tuladan in the Hindi language means charity by weighing the human body. He also quoted the Prophet's teaching that charity rejects or turns away every calamity. The Nizam obviously believed in all these superstitions, like most of the population.

The said ceremony was performed a day prior to the Nizam's twenty-eighth birthday. The Nizam was weighed thrice. The faces of nine stars of the heaven were painted on various metals and they were hung along with rice, kunjid, (a kind of vegetable), pulses and grains arranged in log plates, following the Hindu customs. Different types of costly clothes, like brocades, coarse carpets, blankets, satins and fur coats, were arranged in various columns.

Innumerable pearls were sacrificed on this occasion.The bags of gold were given in reward most benevolently in order to reduce the effect of Mercury. To counteract the effect of Venus, a diamond was decorated, as it wan found to be superior to silver. Similarly, for Mars, corals were heaped; for Jupiter, Pukhraj was given, and Neelam for Saturn. Besides these, Zeb, lead, black oil, etc. were also used. All these were sacrificed on the royal head. After the weighing ceremony, the king adorned a new dress. All the items mentioned above, including grains, clothes, pearls, gold, diamonds and other precious stones, were distributed to the poor[14].

The fact should not be ignored that Hyderabad, which was governed by the Asaf Jahi rulers, consisted of different communities and classes. They never built up a confrontationalist mentality. It is a fact that ignorant, mischievous, and foolish men fight over religious differences. Hyderabad never projected itself either as a Hindu or a Muslim religious and cultural centre. It was the synthesis of both religions. It is essential to build a feeling of common nationality and culture for the progress of a State and country. Mir Mahbub Ali Khan was the finest example of one who always believed in religious cultural harmony.

Though tuladan is a Hindu religious ceremony, the Nizam readily accepted the request of Bansi Raja to perform it in the palace. So Bansi Raja also cited the teachings of the Prophet that charity rejects or turns away every calamity. The tuladan of the Nizam is the finest example of the 'Hyderabadi' culture and eclecticism.Similarly, chayadan was performed on 'the occasion of the solar eclipse on 2nd September 1894 and the lunar eclipse in 1895[15].

Bansi Raja submitted the list of alms to be given to the poor on these occasions. His Highness sanctioned it and accordingly it was distributed. Beside religious ceremonies at the royal palace, social ceremonies were very common and were performed on a grand scale. Bansi Raja would arrange food grains, costly clothes, jewellery and necessary requisites connected with these social ceremonies in consultation with the Nizam and the Begams. It was customary to submit the list of the required items with cost to Nizam. After obtaining his sanction and alterations, if any, Bansi Raja had to consult either with the mother or grandmother of Nizam-VI.

The birth of a male child in the palace was a day to celebrate on a grand scale. The firing of artillery near the royal palace was the indication of the birth of a male child. Distribution of sweets and alms was a common feature. The day was observed as a government holiday and rejoicing in the palace would continue for several days. The naming ceremony, Bismillah Khani, and circumcision ceremony were the days of rejoicing, and ostentation was typical of the royal family and the Hyderabad aristocracy.

The circumcision ceremony had its own importance. On the instructions of Sir Salar Jung, the circumcision ceremony of Mir Mahbub Ali Khan, Nizam-VI was performed in 1874. At the time of the ceremony, the young Nizam was made to sit on the lap of Mustahkam Jung, a companion of Nizam. After the ceremony Mustahkam Jung was awarded a diamond sarpatti with Jigah and precious cloth. The person who performed this ceremony was given fourteen pairs of brocade and one costly doshala[16].

The birthday ceremony of the Nizam had its own significance. Bansi Raja had to play a very important role in organising many functions and rituals, both religious and social, such as: mehndi, ratjaga, dhamal, niaz, jahaz, etc. in the palace on this auspicious occasion.

The mehndi ceremony was usually held on the night before a birthday, engagement or marriage. On the occasion of his birthday, the Nizam sent a letter to Raja Girdhari Pershad that he should arrange mehndi in large quantity since he would like to participate in the mehndi ceremony.

Ratjaga was performed prior to the birthday celebration. It was a night of Prayers and religious rituals. During the jahaz ceremony paper boats decorated with brocades were disposed of in the river at night. Another ceremony which was particularly arranged on the occasion of birthday and marriage was dhamal. In this ceremony, the darwesh used to jump on the fire.

The manja ceremony had a significant place in these place social rituals. The manja was performed at the time of marriage both between Hindus and between Muslims, which prescribes the application of turmeric powder with oil on the body of bride and bridegroom.

But the manja ceremony celebrated at the Royal Place of Asaf Jahs was entirely different. It applied to the gifts presented to Nizarns from the aristocracy to the common man. Each manja was sent In accordance with the rank and status of the sender. Manjas sent from the leading members of the Hyderabad nobility were valued at from twenty thousand to half a lakh of rupees. Every evening processions exhibiting rich presents, clothes, jewellery, sweetmeats, garlands passed through the streets of Hyderabad to the Nizam's palace. In the event of the Prime Minister or Peshkar or any member of Paigah family honouring the procession, a portion of the Nizams troops, nobles, and principal officials escorted them, along with troops, carriages, naubat, roshan chowki and taifa. On the birth of his first daughter, Nizam Unnisa Begam, Nizam-VI received one hundred and one manjas including the manja of Raja Girdhari Pershad[17].

Mir Mahbub Ali Khan instructed Girdbari Pershad that he should be at the palace with flowers and other preparations to receive the manja of Iqbal-ud-Daula, Viqar-ul-Mulk.During 1884, the birthday of the Nizam was celebrated. The celebrations were reported in the local and outside newspapers Special jaridas (gazettes) with detailed programmes were issued. On this auspicious occasion, nobles and dignitaries arranged tea parties at their homes, and the gentry arranged illuminations on their houses. Arches and bunting were used for decoration. All the official buildings including charminar were illuminated. The Regular forces, the Hyderabad Imperial Service and Jamiat-i-Mahbub presented a guard of honour. Feeding of the poor was arranged and alms were distributed.

On this Occasion, a Mughlai Darbar was organised in which sandal paste was applied on the neck of the Nizam. Thereafter the birthday knot was tied and Bansi Raja presented garlands to the Nizam, warphare was performed and nazrs were offered. The Nizam offered garlands to all the nobles who attended the function.

The Nizam-VI used to invite both Hindu and Muslim nobles on the eve of Holi. This colourful Hindu festival was celebrated on a grand scale either at Purani Haveli or Aftab Mahal. Bansi Raja as usual made the necessary arrangements. Besides arranging the various religious and social ceremonies and rituals connected with the royal Palace, Bansil.Raja had the privilege of arranging and organising marriages in the royal palace. While organising the marriages, Bansi Raja not only had to consult the Nizam and report the day-to-day progress, but he had to consult and be in constant touch with the Begams of the palace. Bansi Raja also had the opportunity of making the entire arrangements for the marriages of three successive Paigah family members who had matrimonial alliances with the Ruling family.

The entire arrangements for the marriage of Parwarish Unriisa Begam, daughter of Afzal-ud-Daula,_ Nizam-V, at the

Royal Palace, Were made by Bansi Raja during 1889. She was married to Nawab Bashir-ud-Daula Asman Jah of the Paigah family, who later became the Prime Minister in 1887. The marriage was performed on a grand scale, since the families of the Nizams and the Paigah were equally matched. The marriage was a scene of pomp and grandeur. In accordance with rank and status the Paigah family was next to the Ruling family and had the privilege of matrimonial alliances. Large sums of money and food were given in charity, and the attendants were given costly clothes[19].

In 1872, when the marriage of Jahandar Unnisa Begam, sister of Malibub- Ali Khan, was arranged with Iqbal-ud-Daula of the Paigah family, son of Nawab Rasheeduddin Khan, Amir-i-Kabir-III, who later became the Prime Minister in 1893, Bansi Raja organised all the arrangements from both sides as desired by the ruling family and the family of Paigah. These arrangements includes the arrangement of costly .clothes, jewellery, food, tora or distribution of food, alms, fireworks, etc., and all the ceremonies connected with the marriage. Due to the sincere efforts of Bansi Raja, the marriage was performed on a grand scale. He was in the palace right from the commencement of the various ceremonies of the marriage until the completion of the marriage.

Similarly, Bansi Raja made all arrangements for the marriage of Siraj Unnisa Begam, daughter of Afzal-ud-Daula, with Asaf yawar-ul- Mulk, great-grandson of Sikander Jah Nizam-Ill, during 1879. in this marriage, Bansi Raja made arrangements at the Royal Palace as well as on behalf of the groom.

Bansi Raja not only helped the Nizam find a suitable match for his sister, Najeeb Unnisa, and he relieved Sir Khursheed Jah a Paigah noble, of his anxiety about the rumours of the proposed marriage of Najeeb Unnisa Begam with his son Imam

Jung by finalising it according to the wishes of the Nizam. Bansi Raja was consulted by Khursheed Jah in the preparation of the marriage arrangements at every stage during 1892, a coincidence and a unique opportunity indicative of the trust and confidence the Nizams and the Paigah nobles had in Bansi Raja.

This marriage was also performed on a grand scale. As usual, Bansi Raja made all the arrangements right from the commencement of the preparation of the marriage and the dowry, the engagement ceremony, namakchashi, distribution of tora, ratjaga, jahaz, haldi, dhamal, niaz, sarnchaq, mehndi, sehra, barat, rukhsal, chowthi, hiljan and jumagi (Five Fridays).

While narrating the arrangements about the said marriage, Bansi Raja wrote that Mir Mahbub Ali Khan had not only maintained the pomp, splendour and tradition of the Asaf Jahi dynasty and Asaf Jahi rulers, but in munificence and benevolence there was no match for Mahbub Ali Khan; the alms were generously distributed, unlocking the Royal Treasury, which continued over days and nights for a long time. Gold, silver and pearls were showered on the public. It is said that the people of Hyderabad had not seen such a lavish and generous shower of gold in their lives and would remember this for years to come.

Conclusion

Bansi Raja was thus the most influential and key figure in the Nizam's court. He played a leading role in making arrangements and organising festivals and all the ceremonies connected with the birth, marriages and deaths in the Nizam's palace. Since most of his functions were connected with the court and, palace, he had to spend most of his time there. He was assigned important responsibilities within the court and the management of the Nizam's household functions. In the process he maintained old customs in vogue at the court of the Mughal Kings and from the times of Asaf Jah-I. His role was recognised through personal letters and subsequently the visit by the Nizam Mir Mahbub Ali Khan to his palace. It is well known that distinguished personalities emerged in Hyderabad. But impartial historians will agree that Nawab Mir Mahbub Ali Khan Nizam-VI and Sir Salar Jung-I were the only two among them who acquired the distinction of being acclaime 'men of destiny', The people of Hyderabad, even today, respect Nizam-VI as a secular ruler, who lived with the people in every sense of the term. Sir Salar Jung-I was a versatile personality, a renowned administrator and reformer of great calibre. Writing the biography of a person who was very closely associated with these two distinguished personalities was a formidable task.

NOTES

1. NAI, FD no -467 memorandum by Major Euan smith, first Assistant Resident, Hyderabad, dt 10th August 1876.P5.
2. The chronology of Modern Hyderabad, Central Records office Hyderabad, 1954 P VI.
3. Raja Girdhari pershed, daily Dairy 1894, P 24.
4. Raja Girdhari pershed, daily Dairy 1894, PP 29-30.
5. Raja Girdhari pershed, daily Dairy 1894, P 31.
6. Syed Abid Hassan, Whiter Hyderbad,Hyderabad, 1935, P. 98.
7. Col.Nawab Sir Afsar-ul-mulk, Swameti Afsari, Nizam-ul-Matabe,Hyderabad. 1901 PP 62-86.
8. Raja Girdhari Pershad, Travel No VIII PP 128-130.
9. Hyderabad Affairs, vol. III op cit., PP 486-487.
10. Raja Girdhari Pershad, op cit., Travel No.11, PP 184-186.
11. Programme of the visit of H.E. the Viceroy at Hyderabad, 3rd, November, 1892.

12. Jeevan yar Jung,op.cit., P.136.
13. Raja Girdhari Pershad, Daily Dairy-1893, P 58.
14. Raja Girdhdri Pershad, Daily Diary-1894, PP 27-28.
15. Raja Girdhdri Pershad, Daily Diary-1894, PP 13.
16. Raja Girdhdri Pershad, op.Cit P 96.
17. Raja Girdhari Pershad Daily Diary-1883, PP20-21.
18. Raja Girdhari Pershad Daily Diary-1883, PP 50-51.
19. Raja Girdhari Pershad.Op.Cit., P73.

CHAPTER – 4

Dalit Organisations in Erstwhile Hyderabad State: The Cause of *Dalit* Liberation

AKULAPALLY KUMARASWAMY

Introduction

India has witnessed many movements from the late 19th century to the mid-20th century. While some of them were revolutionary movements, some were political and yet some others were social movements. Each of these movements had its own well-defined objectives to accomplish which the organisers endeavoured relentlessly. Among the social movements, Dalit movements like Bahujan and Mahar movements in Marathwada, Ezhava Movement in Kerala, Self-Respect Movement in Tamil Nadu and those in Andhra and the Hyderabad State are a class apart and are notable ones. The present paper of mine attempts to present a perspective of the socio-political profiles, and the ideologies and perceptions of the leadership spearheading the Dalit movements that took place in the erstwhile Hyderabad State, their objectives, and achievements.

The Hyderabad State was under the rule of Mughals until the Nizam-ul-Mulk Asaf Jah, a *Subedar* under the Mughal ruler, established an independent kingdom in 1724. The State was under the rule of Nizam-ul-Mulk and his descendants up to

1948. The State witnessed many *Dalit* movements that carried the aim of eradicating child-marriages, Jogini and Matangi systems, black magic and such other social evils prevalent among the so-called untouchables. The present study aims to discuss such *Dalit* movements led by Manyasangam, Jaganmitramandali, Deccan Humanitarian league, Swastikdal, Sunitha Balasamajam, Arundateeyasabha, Manavaseva samithi, Depressed class Association, Scheduled Castes Federations, Adi Hindu Mahasabha, and Matanga Mahasabha. The primary aim of the study is to discuss the details of such movements.

Jagan Mitra Mandali

Bhagyareddy Varma started the Jagan Mitra Mandali in 1906 in Hyderabad (there is a controversy over his being the Founder-President of the Mandali),[1] with the objective of educating the so-called untouchables and to bring about social consciousness among them. As a part of this effort, he regularly organised Harikatha programmes, at the beginning and end of which, he used to address them with inspiring speeches. He vested all his energies in bringing about awareness on the social stigmas surrounding the untouchables. The members of Jagan Mitra Mandali followed the precepts of Buddha, while at the same time adored the Vedic Dharma. They propagated vegetarianism.[2] During the years 1913 to 1938, they have celebrated the Buddha's birthday on the Full-moon day (Pournami) of the second month of the Hindu calendar (Vaisakha masam).[3] The Mandali regularly organised a programme called Preeti Bhoanam, where people dined together along with the untouchables.[4]

Manya Sangham

Bhagyareddy Varma started the Manya Sangham in 1911. He renamed it as Adi Hindu Social Service League in 1922, through which he strived towards the eradication of alcoholism, animal sacrifices, temples, evil practices, child marriages and such other social evils. On 13th January 1913 the General Committee of the organisation elected an Executive Committee to work towards achieving its goals.

Swastik Dal

In 1925 when Hyderabad was affected by plague again, it was the Swastik Dal that came to the rescue of patients who were left to fend themselves. The volunteers of Dal served them in time with humane touch and their efforts were widely appreciated. The members of the Dal have served with the same dedication at the conference organised by National Congress at Kakinada and at a public meeting at Gudiwada.[5] In 1932 Bhagyareddy Varma started the Swastik Dal comprising of 35 members from the Dalit communities. The Dal served the plague affected citizens of Hyderabad and was awarded the Maharaja Kishen Pershad Silver Medal for its services. The main objective of Swastik Dal was to eradicate cruelty to animals. Bhagyareddy was a whole-time Director of the Dal. The Dal worked on the twin principles of socialism and humanitarianism. In a way, it worked like the Red Cross Society. The yellow Swastik, a Buddhist icon, was the symbol of the Dal. When the city of Hyderabad and its surroundings were affected by plague and cholera, the activists of the Dal rendered selfless service to the suffering people[6]. Between 1906 and 1916, Bhagyareddy travelled around the State of Hyderabad organising cultural activities, especially Harikathas, addressed numerous gatherings, thus kindling the fires of rebellion among the untouchables. Through numerous programmes organised under the aegis of Bhajan Mandali, the Swastik Dal (voluntary organisation) and with close relations with humanists among the upper-caste

Hindus, Bhagyareddy Varma succeeded to a major extent in eradicating social evils like Devadasi, Basivini and Jogini systems besides alcoholism.[7]

Sunitha Balasamajam

Social reformation activities first by starting Suneethi Bala Samajamu at Kummariguda, his place of residence in Secunderabad. Although an alcoholic himself, he got rid of the intemperance and strove to propagate for a ban on alcoholism, eradication of the Jogini system and black magic activities.[8] Ramaswamy sought refuge in Mandippa Hanumantha Rao, a spiritual Guru who preached under the name of Achalabodha, and under the Guru's influence turned a pure vegetarian. By 1912 Suneethi Bala Samajam gained good popularity. He started Manava Seva Samithi in 1922 to launch his social service activities in a big way. The speeches he gave on behalf of the Samithi were in total contradiction to those he gave on behalf of Jatiyonnati Sabha. They launched Ahimsa movement seeking eradication of animal sacrifices in front of temples. In 1923 he organised a meeting of Jatiyonnati Sabha, to which he invited Bhagyareddy. But, the latter issued a press notification stating that Jatiyonnati Sabha was an offshoot of his own organisation, leading to differences of opinion between Ramaswamy and Bhagyareddy.[9] To put an end to the atrocities of the Choudharies, in 1924 he invited C. V. Padma Rao as a representative of Government, to join hands. He spread the activities of Jatiyonnati Sabha in various areas like Ghasmandi, Nallagutta, Regimental Bazar, Ramakrishnapuram, in the city. He was severely critical of Bhagyareddy Varma's support to Malas. Ramaswamy strived hard to bring-in consciousness among the Madigas. He oversaw many inter-caste marriages. During the summer of 1925, Ramaswamy was on duty at

Secunderabad Railway Station on a Sunday, when he was informed that some people are about to offer a Dalit girl as sacrifice to appease gods in the forested area of Kavadiguda, he rushed to the spot, saved the girl and handed-over the culprits to the police. This news spread across the city like wild fire popularising him all the more.

Arundathiya Mahasabha

Realising that the Malas have awaken, to usher in a similar consciousness among the Madigas for their uplift Ramaswamy started Adi Arundhatiya Mahasabha on 1st June 1931, with Suravaram Pratapa Reddy as the Founder President. Fearing that it is detrimental to the cause of Dalits if the Malas and Madigas fight separately, Arigay approached Bhagyareddy with the proposal for a united fight. Bhagyareddy not only rejected the proposal, but had also convinced Ramaswamy that a separate association to protect the interests of Madigas is the need of the hour. Unable to spend whole time on employment because of his social activities, he resigned and dedicated whole time towards the Dalit movement.[10]

Sangabhivriddi Samajam

Madari Audiah was a great *Dalit* social reformer. Manyasangham started by Bhagyareddy in Ghasmandi was under his administration. He endeavoured to annihilate the blind beliefs that have strongly rooted themselves among the *Dalits*. He strove hard in dissuading them from drinking and eating meat. He had himself started an organisation *Sanghabivruddhi Samajam* for the development of society, through which he continued his endeavours to annihilate alcoholism and meat consumption among the *Dalits* and at the same time, to educate them he started a school in 1906 that had an initial strength of 15 students. He appointed a teacher to teach these students. Later on, Dewan Bahadur Padmarao Mudaliar became the Honorary Secretary of the school, who acquired land from the then Resident Sir William Barton and built a permanent building.[11] The school was then renamed after Sir William Barton. Audiah built a temple dedicated to Chennakesava Swami to enable the *Dalits* offer prayers.

Depressed Class Student Union

The Conference of Depressed Classes Students' Union held between 18th and 20th July, 1942 at Parbhani, presided over by him is of historical significance. When B.S. Venkat Rao was elected as Education Minister in the Nizam's government in 1947, Syamsunder was elected as the President of Depressed Classes Association. He stood beside Ittehadul Muslimeen when there was anger among the people against the Muslim rule. During those days, Syamsunder along with B.S. Venkat Rao supported the Nizam's declaration that the Hyderabad State would remain independent and would not be integrated into Union of India. He deplored the induction of Congress supporters into the ministries by Khasim Rizwi. He blamed Rizwi of pushing the *Dalits* to live under servitude to the Hindus. Yet, he went on to proclaim that the *Dalits* are safe only in the Nizam's dominion. For three years Syamsunder represented 10 million *Dalits* as a member of Scheduled Castes' Welfare Fund. Dalits must be given freedom in social, economic and education sectors (5) we want a citizenship that gives us peace and equality. These slogans gained immense popularity during those days.

Aryasamaj

Arya Samaj strives to extricate the Dalits from untouchability and blind beliefs. He began his social reformation activities in

1930 and endeavoured to educate the untouchables, drive away their blind beliefs and unsanitariness, and to persuade them to abstain meat. He purchased lands in Hyderabad with his own money and donated them for construction of homes for Dalits Pandit R. Laxmaiah belonged to the Madiga community and retired from the Forests Division. Post retirement, he converted to become an Arya Samajist and participated in the Dalit movements. Gentle and amicable in nature towards all, he participated in the Dalit movement as a follower of Arigay Ramaswamy. Recognising his services, Arya Samaj honoured him with the title Pandit. He organised meetings for the benefit of Dalits to explain the precautions to be taken to escape bombing attacks during the Second World War.[12]

Matangajanasabha

In 1925 the Matanga Jana Sabha was started under the aegis of Matanga community leader Guntimalla Ramappa. The organisation was started to dissuade the community people from consuming meat and alcoholic drinks on both auspicious and inauspicious occasions besides discouraging them from following the tradition of converting young girls as Matangis. They persuaded the community to send their children to either Adi Hindu run schools or those of the government. They have organised a massive public meeting at Nampally Road on 2nd March 1932 and infused consciousness in the Matanga community. People in large numbers gathered for the meeting.[13]

Arundhateeya Yuvajana Mrityu Sahakara Sangham

Some of the youth of Arundhateeya Mahasabha have volunteered to stand by the families of deceased people of the community by starting the Arundhateeya Yuvajana Mrityu Sahakara Sangham. Mudigonda Veeraswamy and Bhuchala Swamy were elected

President and Secretary of the Sangham. During those days there were more deaths due to plague, cholera and alcoholism. The Sangham came to the aid of the families not only economically but also got the children enrolled into schools.[14]

Conclusion

As part of the social reformation movements that have started across India during the first decade of 19th century to the mid-20th century, South India including the Erstwhile State of Hyderabad too witnessed a slew of movements in that direction. Of these movements, the Dalit movements in the state are a class apart as they were started by Dalit activists who were educated in the institutions set up either by the Nizam's government or by Christian Missionaries. With the education they have acquired, they became conscious of the society around them and started setting up reformist organisations according to their ideologies and objectives and aimed at annihilation of many social evils like child-marriages, black magic, Jogini and Matangi system, alcoholism prevalent among the Dalits, besides bringing-in an awareness of cleanliness in them. In their endeavours to usher-in a sense of self-respect, thereby a social transformation among the so-called untouchables the Dalit activists have dedicated their lives. In the process the Dalits have a new realistic perspective of life and started fighting for it. The spirit of such leaders still continues to this day and laid down the path for future of Dalit consciousness.

NOTES

1. Chinna Rao Yagati., *Andhra Pradesh Dalitodyama Charthra (1900-1950)*, Hyderabad Book Trust, Hyderabad, 2007, p. 110.
2. Sanjay Pashwan & Pramanshi Jaideva., (Ed), *Encyclopedia of Dalits in India*, Vol- IV, Kalpak Publications, Delhi, 2004, p.192.

3. Goutham M.B., *Bhagyodayam, Samanthara Prachuranalu,* Hyderabad, 2009, p.97.
4. Ibid, p. 27.
5. Chinna Rao Yagati., *Andhra Pradesh Dalitodyama Charthra (1900-1950),* Op.cit, p. 112.
6. Venkata Swamy P. R., *Ma* Vimukthi *Poratam,* Ambedkar Publications Society, Hyderabad, 2003, p. 19.
7. Ibid, pp. 111-113.
8. Sanjay Pashwan & Pramanshi Jaideva., (Ed), *Encyclopedia of Dalits in India,* Vol- IV, Op.cit,, p. 183.
9. Gail Omved., *Dalit and the Democratic Revolution, Dr. Ambedkar and the Dalit Movement in Colonial India,* Sage Publications, New Delhi, 1994, p.122.
10. Ibid, pp. 36.
11. Goutham M.B., *Bhagyodayam, Samanthara Prachuranalu,* Op.cit,, pp. 19-22.
12. Ibid, pp. 52-53.
13. Venkata Swamy P. R., *Ma Vimukthi Poratam,* Op.cit, pp. 76.

CHAPTER – 5

Art and Architecture Under the Asafjahis : A Study on Palaces

S. VENKATARATNAM

Introduction

The Hyderabad state was founded by Nizam – ul – Mulk in the year 1724. The period of the Asaf Jahis rule in Hyderabad from 1724 to 1948. During the long period of the Nizams in the Hyderabad, they were served by Diwans and prime ministers. Hyderabad state comprised regions of Karnataka and Maharashtra. During the Asaf Jahis time the architecture was different from the Qutub Shahis architecture. Under Asaf Jahis rule, Hyderabad state seen all round development and created its own identity in India in the fields of culture, language literature and particularly art and architecture. The architecture of Asaf Jahis may be classified into places of the Nizams and the royality, Government and public buildings, Tombs and mosques and places of the chief Nobles. My paper particularly to covered the palaces in Hyderabad and another construction.

The Falakhnuma Palace

The Falakhnuma Palace the foundation stone for the construction was laid by Sir Vicar on 1884 March 3. It took nine years to complete the construction and Furnish the palace.

The Falakhnuma Palace also known as "Mirror of Sky". This is the most magnificent and splendid palaces of the world. It was originally built by a paigah nobleman. The palace was built and furnished at a cost of Four million rupees, which necessitated borrowing money from the Bank of Bengal. The Sixth Nizam of Hyderabad, Mir Mahaboob Ali Khan was invited to stay at the palace. The Nizam used the palace as a guest house for the royal guests visiting the Kingdom of Hyderabad. The Falakhnuma Palace constructed with European style. In the palace the drawing room in two portions. Europeans visiting Hyderabad were usually lodged in Falakhnuma palace and special room were prepared for special guests. The palace in an estate 300 acres, was reached by a winding road passing through a large gateway magnificent in design. The distinguished guests who were accommodated in this palace were king George V of England Queen Mary, Prince and Princess of Wales etc.

The Paigah Palaces

The Paigah Palace was built by Sir Vicar-ul-Umra, a paigah noble man. This was built after he gave the famous Falakhnuma Palace to the Sixth Nizam of Hyderabad state, Mahabub Ali Khan Asaf Jah VI. The word paigah which means pomp and rank in Persian. Their palaces were built in close proximity of the Nizam's original palaces at Chau Mahala. These palaces were of Sir Asman Jah, Sir Khurshid Jah and Sir Vaqarul Umara. The palace of Asman Jah was one of the oldest and most beautiful. It was built in original Mushal style by Nawab Shamsul Umra. Vicar-ul-Umra's palace lies further south of the earlier paigah palaces.

King Kothi Palace

The King Kothi palace was constructed by Kamal Khan and sold to Nizam ones he expressed his desire for the palace. The young Nizam moved in when he was only 13 years. In this sprawling residence, the heir apparent was installed in the charge of Sir Brias Egerton. The estate later came to be known as 'King Kothi', for the intitials KK of its original owner it bore could not be erased from very nook and corner of the palace. The palace in which the Nizam VII lived was called Nazri Bagh. The Nizam VII very closed to the king kothi palace. The sons and grandsons of the Nizams and other members of royal family were lived in other palaces.

Salar Jungs Palaces

Salar Jungs Palace is a historic palace having accommodated many generations of the prime ministers of Hyderabad state. At first the this palace of Nawab Mir Abul Qasim. Mir Alam Bahadur Prime Minister and later it was occupied by his son in law, Nawab Muneer ul mulk. Who succeeded Mir Alam as Prime minister. Later it was occupied by Salar Jung – I the grandson of Mir Alam. The palace comprised eight blocks of buildings. This palace the drawing room was the most important among them. It's architectural design was Persian style, with symmetrical arches wooden pillars with floral decorations topped with carved peacocks. Salarjung occupied this palace, and he made new additions and renovated the entire palace. He built a very specious banquet house called Nayamkan.

The Malwal Palace

The Malwal Palace was built in 1845 and is located at the road leading towards east from Charminar in Hyderabad. This palace constructed in Mughal and Rajasthani style. The palace constructed by Raja Ram pershad lal Bahadur. The beautiful arches of the palace are of lacquered wood. As Raja Shivaraj and his ancestors were the custodians of the revenue records of the provinces of Hyderabad and Bidar. Malwala palace was the only other palace in Hyderabad having a wooden Pavillion.

Purani Haveli Palace

Purani Haveli also called as Masarrat Mahal Palace located in Hyderabad. The Purani Haveli palace was the official residence of the Nizam. It was also known as Haveli Khadeem, which means 'old Mansion', the palace was constructed Sikandar Jah (Asaf Jah-III) by his father Alikhan Bahadur Asaf Jah-II. The Sixth and Seventh Nizams were born at this palace and did spend a part of their life at this palace and did spend a part of their life at this palace. Sikandar Jah (Nizam-III) added a new structure of this palace called 'Aina Khana (House of Mirrors) and Chini Khana (House of Glass or China Ware) Purani Haveli constructed different styles of decoration and furnish in various rooms are there. In this palace having drawing room, study room, rest room, dinning hall. Purani Haveli palace, the Nizam – VI had special chairs manufactured for him. This palace constructed from Oriental to Western that an entire floor and ward – robe on two sides.

Chowmahalla Palace

The Chowmahalla palace built near Charminar in 1750 by Salabat Jung. Chowmahalla means 'Four Palaces'. The group of four palaces was built around a pleasant quadrangular garden with a large marble cistern in the centre and a fountain Jelting water. This palace is the official residence of Nizams. This palace construction completed during the Nizam of Afzal – ud – daula (Asaf Jah – V). The palace is unique for its style and elegance. Chowmalla palaces were meant different purposes. The one was the Durbar hall, the Southern palace the dignitaries and high officials were received. The Western palace was meant for the

Nizam's private residence. The entrance of the Chowmahalla palace was through the palace sequre with a tall arch built in 1748 and which opened on the Lad Bazar side. Salabat Jung describes Chowmahalla palace it is a second block of houses also a great hall, celling was supported by a number of wooden pillars each of a single piece, carpeted and one storeyed. The chowmahalla palace constructed later Mughal, an Oriental version of renaissance Indo – Saracenic arches and Mughal tower and turrets predominated. White marbles steps led to the hall through these arches. The hall itself was in marble, open towards the garden on one side, but enclosed on the other three sides.

Tombs and Mosques

During Asaf Jahis time the construction of Tombs and Mosques are important one. The Asaf Jahi tombs are situated at Macca Masjid compound. They built as arched gallery of stone at the southern end of the mosque or on the left side before the main structure of the Mecca Masjid. The tomb of the first Asaf Jah, Nizam – ul – Mulk is at Khuldabad in Aurangabad, while the remains of the last Nizam Mir Osman Ali Khan are at Judi Mosque near King Kothi. During the Asaf Jahi time, there are many mosques constructed in different places as when toms are constructed.

Conclusion

During the period of Asaf Jahis occupied Unique places in the art and architecture. Nizams constructed many palaces in Hyderabad and also constructed Mir Alam's Baradar – lakkar kot also known as wooden palace near bank river of "Musi Baradari of Maharaja Chandulal laid foundation on 1822, Fakhrul mulk's palace, Raja Dhanrajgiri palace are another construction in Hyderabad. Nizams using construction styles called Indo-Sarsanic, Persian styles, European styles, Indo – Rajasthani style. This paper to covered the most palaces in Hyderabad and other constructions. Asaf Jahi in the period of last two Nizams art and architecture depicts the ideas and thoughts of the people and culture and civilization. In Hyderabad another constructions called Osmania University, hospital were built in Mughal and – Indo – Saracenic style. The High Court was built in Indo – Saracenic style, the legislative assembly is constructed in the style of Saracenic – Rajastani style. The city improvement board was setup this time to look after, and laid the gardens, markets, streets etc.

REFERENCES

1. Ali Cheragh, Moulavi, Hyderabad Under SalarJung (4 vols)
2. Gray, Basil, The Arts of India.
3. Nayeem, M.A., Asaf Jahi period–Architectural Heritage : Golconda, Hyderabad, 1975.
4. Singh, S. Nihal, The Nizam and the British empire.
5. Regani, Sarojini, Nizam – British relations 1724 – 1857.
6. V.K. Bawa, The Last Nizam life and times of Mir Osman Alikhan.
7. Sherwani H.K., History of Medieval Deccan, 1974.
8. Raza Ali Khan, Hyderabad 400 years.
9. Muttalib M.A., Administration of Justice under the Nizams(1724-1948),Andhra Pradesh.
10. Briggs H.G., The Nizam, his history and his relations with the British, London, 1861.

CHAPTER – 6

Political Parties and Profile of the Political Leadership among the Toddy Tappers in Andhra Pradesh

P. MUTHYAM

The movement of the toddy tappers in the post-independent period in Andhra Pradesh has two dimensions. One was to liberate them from exploitation of the feudal domination and age old colonial and Nizam policies and the other was to improve their low economic status and political predicament and give them a say in politics. The tappers began to agitate and their leadership gave them a hope that something could be done to remedy their position. The secular leaders systematically worked for greater politicisation of the community and spearheaded the movement focusing over issue after another. Soon after independence the toddy tappers reacted to their oppressive conditions by forming an association based on cast identity in Andhra Pradesh. The formation of the Gouda Sangha is especially noteworthy in this period. It was formed in 1955 in the Hyderabad state with the toddy tappers of Nalgonda, Khammam, Warangal, Karimnagar, West Godavari, East Godavari, Krishna, The Andhra Toddy tappers and Workers Federation was actively working during the same period. In this stage there was not much interaction among the cast associations in Andhra and in Telangana.

Soon after independence the toddy tappers transcended their caste identity and felt the need to organise more on the issue of the rights of the toddy tappers then on their caste solidarity. In this stage the political organisation of the leadership whether a Congress, Communists or Praja Socialist Party were over looked. All those who felt victimised joined together inspite of their regional and ideological proclivities. The exploitative nature of the excise policies, the new political atmosphere, the rise of the political consciousness, formation of separate linguistic state in 1957 helped in uniting the toddy tappers from all the regions to form a state level organization. The power brokers and contractors within the Gouda community offered resistance to the formation of a state level organisation as they perceived this as a threat to their control and leadership.

The first and foremost factor is the formation of the Andhra Pradesh Toddy Tappers and Workers Federation and the Council for the Protection of the Rights of the Toddy Tapping professionals and Industrialists which acted as lobbies and pressure groups. The political activities of these organizations created a sort of political consciousness among the scattered toddy tappers all over the state, which ultimately led unity among them. These are the organizations which have effectively articulated the interests of the tappers. The pamphlets, booklets, the speeches of the leaders in the conferences made them conscious about their interests.

The second factor is the introducing of the policy of Toddy Toppers Co-operative Societies and the policy of 'Tree for Tapper' and the total abolition of the auction system. All the three policies have brought about the socio-economic conditions of the toddy tappers. With the introduction of new toddy policies some *lakhs* of people who depended for their survival on the age old toddy tapping occupation became independent of the feudal landlords who were contractors of the toddy. Now they are free from bondage. The new policies, have thus given them an opportunity to strengthen their social-economic and political position.

The third factor is the recognition of the strength of the toddy tappers by all the political parties. They constitute around 20 or 21% in the total population of Andhra Pradesh and second largest community among the backward classes. Since one of the aspects of the modern electoral politics is to be base their calculations on vote bank around community solidarity and identity it is inevitable to the political parties to take into account the votes of the tappers as a community.

The last but not the least factor is the nature of political system itself. Since the dawn of independence, the frame work of India's politics have been the liberal democratic parliamentary system ensuring adult franchise and equal opportunity to all citizens to participate in politics. This has integrated the marginalised sections among the toddy tapper into mainstream politics. They have become conscious and are no longer willing to play a docile role. They have recognised their role as voters in a representative democracy. The education middle class among them have emerged as their leaders to them and inspire them to take part in ongoing political process.

Toddy Tappers: Leadership Profile of the Communist Party of Indian

The toddy tappers have been mobilized through their pressure groups like Andhra Pradesh Toddy Tappers and Workers Federation while taking guidance from the Communist Party of India. More specifically the toddy tappers in the Telangana region actively participated in the communist movement activities started in 1940s, when it initiated a militant rebellion against the feudal domination of the Nizam region in the Hyderabad state. As a part of the overall rural mass uprising the toddy tappers also raised their arms against the Nizam rule. Since the toddy trees were an important source of excise revenue. The workers began to cut down toddy trees. This was also a symbolic defiance and partly used as a propaganda against toddy-drinking. This act was also influenced by Gandhian ethics and Congress Party politics which advocated prohibition. Most of the toddy tappers reached against the cutting of trees, since it denied them their day to day livelihood. The Communists, too later realized that by cutting down toddy trees they were depriving a great many active members of their own dalams and Sanghas their livelihood, and gave the slogan of 'Trees for Tappers', corresponding to the slogan of 'Land to the Tillers'.

Mr. Dharmabiksham member of the CPI, belonging to the toddy tappers community played a prominent role in organizing the toddy tappers since them. As a student he joined Andhra Mahasabha and subsequently he entered the Communist movement in 1942. After independence he has been continuously elected as a member of legislative assembly Nalgonda constituency representing the Communist Party of India. In 1957 when the Andhra Pradesh Toddy Tappers and Workers Federation were started, he was elected its president. In the All India Toddy Tappers and Workers Federation in 1978 too he was elected as its president. In 1990 and he was elected as a Member of Parliament from Nalgonda parliamentary Constituency on behalf of C.P.I. Likewise Mr. Desinichinna Mallaiah, who has been an active worker in the Andhra Pradesh Toddy Tappers and Workers Federation and a member of C.P.I. from Warangal district was also elected as M.L.A. on the Communist party of India ticket in 1995. Under their leadership the toddy tappers have been associated with Communist Party of India and the later strongly put fourth their demands. The toddy tappers thus are a consistent vote bank of the C.P.I. in Khammam, Warangal, Nalgonda, Rangareddy, Nizambad, Adilabad districts.

Toddy Toppers: Congress party and its Leaders

The electoral participation of the toddy tappers started during colonial period under the banner of the Congress Party. Mr. K.E. Madanna, who belonged to the toddy tappers community in Kurnool, was elected for the first time in 1938 as the District Board member. While defeating Mr. Subba Reddy. He soon acquired a base not only among the backward and weaker sections at the grass root level but also with Mr. T. Prakasham Panthulu who encouraged Mr. Madanna to participate in the nationalist movement. He organised meetings like non-cooperation, civil disobedience, and so on. He soon became a popular leader in Kurnool district of Rayalaseema. He started organising the rural illiterate, poor, to struggle against the violence and inequality perpetuated by the upper caste Reddy feudal lords. Mr. Madanna actively participated and mobilized the toddy tappers in support of the movement led by Mr. Gouth Lachanna to lift the prohibition on toddy in 1950s. Later Mr. Madanna himself emerged as a powerful toddy contractor. He played a significant role in helping Mr. Sanjeevayya win on behalf of Congress party in all the three assembly election held in 1962, 1967, 1972. The election in Kurnool constituency represented by Sanjivayya was seen as a virtual competition between Mr. K.E. Madanna and Mr. K. Vijaya Bhaskar Reddy. Since independence Madanna had been continuously elected to the local bodies for the post of councillor, member of Municipality and Zilla Parishad. In 1978 he was elected as a Member of legislative Council to the Andhra Pradesh. Simultaneously in

1978 his eldest son K.E. Krishna Murthy was elected as M.L.A. on Congress party ticket from Dhone Constituency and soon became legislative secretary. In 1980 he was appointed Minster for Excise, in 1981 and elected Chairman of Kurnool Zilla Parishad. In 1983 he was re-elected as M.L.A from the same constituency.

Mr. K.E. Madanna started as an organiser at the grass root level and was soon inducted into the factional strife of the Congress Party. His main rival in the factional politics of the rayalaseema Congress was Mr. Vijaya Bhasker Reddy. At the same time he acquired an economic status as a toddy contractor. His son Mr. K.E. Krishna Murthy was inducted. In a row several family members acquired important positions even in the Telugu Desam Party. This is a typical example of a dedicated worker in pre-independent politics, being sucked in to the factional strife of ruling party politics, even graduating to the position of a Minister, but losing touch with the base.

Similarly other leaders who have been elected on the Congress Party tickets are Mr. V. Mallikarjun Goud, Member of Parliament since 1971, twice from medak constituency and thrice from Mahaboobnagar constituency. He also held a ministerial position as deputy and state Railways and Defence Minister in the cabinet of the Congress Party. He was also at the time the president of the Andhra Pradesh Congress Committee. Further another prominent political leader belonging to the toddy tapper community is Mr. Kudupudi Prabhakar Rao who has been elected as M.L.A. continuously for the last twenty years. He was also a cabinet minister. Yet another example of a prosperous toddy tapper is that of Mr. T. Bala Goud from Ilapuram village of yellaredyy Taluk of Nizambad district. He was elected as Sarpanch of Lingampeta in 1960, when he began his career. He was then elected Panchayat Samithi President In 1970 and M.L.A. from

Yella Reddy constituency in 1978. He successfully worked as minister of Roads and Buildings. Later he was elected Member of Parliament twice from Nizambad constituency on Congress party ticket.

A senior leader of the Congress Party belonging to the toddy tapper community Mr. Vanga Narayana Goud has been active in the congress since the time of nationalist movement. He became the Municipal Chairman of Nagar Kurnool in Mahaboobnagar in 1967. He was elected as an independent M.L.A. in 1972. From 1981 to 1983 he was also the Chairman of Mahaboobnagar Zilla Parishad and again elected as M.L.A. in 1983 on Congress Party ticket. His son Mr. Vanga Mohan Goud was subsequently elected as Sarpanch in 1981 to Nagar Kurnool and during 1989 general election to the Assembly from the same constituency. Mr. Mula Mukesh Goud Began his political career as an activist in the National Students Union of India. Since his college days, he was elected as the students union president of V.V. College, Hyderabad in 1978 and later became to NSUI, General Secretary of the Youth Congress in 1982. He was soon elected as a Corporator to the General Hyderabad Municipality from Jambagh in 1986, and they rose to be elected as an M.L.A. in 1989 on the Congress Party.

Mr. Bandi Narsa Goud was the General Secretary of the Youth Congress and district executive member of the Congress. In 1983 he was elected as Sarpanch on Congress party in Pothareddy Pete of Medak district. Mr. V. Damodar Goud has been elected as the Municipal Chairman on the Congress Party ticket from Bhuvanagiri of Nalgonda district in 1995. Some profile of the mobility of political leaders belonging to the toddy tapper community in the Congress party has been drawn up in detail. These profiles indicate that each of the leaders from the toddy tapper community rose from the ranks. Thus almost all of them began their political careers at grass root level as Sarpanch, Corporators, member of students union or trade unions. From this stage they acquired experience by holding office in larger bodies or as office bearers in the Congress Party at the district and State level. Given their capacity to mobilise voters, organisational skills, and ability to play a role in the factional politics of the Congress Party. They were even given tickets to contest for seats' in the sates in the State Assembly and the parliament. Some of them gad even held ministerial positions in both sate and Central level cabinets. The portfolios given to them were also reasonably important.

These candidates consolidated their power and strength in several ways. They projected other members in their family as the next generation politicians. They amassed wealth through the business of toddy tapping as contractors and become very important power brokers. Given the fact that 'toddy is crucial both as revenue to the state as well as for mustering votes at the time of elections the leaders gained a political clout which could not be matched by any other caste community.

Although significant policy decisions benefiting the 'real' toddy tappers were formulated while most of these leaders were in office, this section of politicians among the toddy tapper community found methods for perpetuating their positions of wealth as contractors going against the very institutional arrangements designed to reach out to the poor among the community.

Toddy Tappers: Leadership Profile in Other Parties

Mr. Gouth Lachanna a freedom fighter, mass leader, politician and crusader of the toddy tapper rights since long belonged to the toddy tappers family of Srikakulam district. Since his childhood he was influenced by the nationalist movement and

Gandhian ideas. As a young patriot he not only mobilised the people to fight against the British imperialist colonial rule through Gandhian methods but also against the domination of the Zamindars in the Northern Coastal Andhra. In order to make the Harijan reform movement as well.

Mr. Lachanna became the State Executive Member of the Congress Socialist Party in 1935. As the general secretary of the inviting Committee of Palasa Conference of the All Indian Kisan Sabha in 1940 he played an active role. He was also the founder president of the Indian National Trade Union Congress of the A.P branch.

In 1948 he was elected as the Member of the Legislative Assembly from the workers constituency of Vishakhapatnam and East Godavari. He was Joint Secretary of the Andhra Congress Committee, later he became the General Secretary of the Krushikar Lok Party in 1951. He was elected as M.L.A. on KLP ticket in 1952 from Sompet constituency. He was also member in the partition committee along with N. Sanjeeva Reddy and T. Viswandham. He was the Labour Minister in the first Andhra Cabinet headed by Prakasham Pantulu. Again in 1955, Lachanna was the labour and Welfare Minister in Mr. B. Gopal Reddy cabinet. After the formation of the state of Andhra Pradesh in 1956, he was the Agricultural and Labour minister in Prakasham Pantulu cabinet.

Mr. Lachanna joined the Swatantra Party as its joint secretary which came into existence in 1958. In 1962, he was the Swatantra party legislative leader. In 1964 and 1968 he was M.L.A. from Sompet and elected as Member of Parliament from Srikakulam constituency as an independent candidate. He was elected as the president of the State Bharatiya Lokdal. He was the vice-president of the Janata Party in 1977. Mr. Gouth Lachanna was not contractors are business man.

Mr. Macharla Jaganadham is a representative of Varadhannapeta constituency of Warangal district. He was elected as M.L.A. for twice from Vardhanapeta. In 1978 on behalf of janata Party and in 1983 on behalf of Congress party ticket. He was also Joint Secretary and the General Secretary of the Andhra Pradesh Congress Party Committee.

Toddy Tappers: leadership Profile in Telugu Desam Party

The Telugu Desam Party came in to being in 1983. One of the vote banks for the T.D.P. is the backward classes. Since the toddy tappers constitute the second largest community among the backward castes the toddy tappers have played a significant role in the Telugu Desam Party, some of the important members from the toddy tappers community in the Telugu Desam Party are given below. Mr. Gouth Shyam Sundar Shivaji has been continuously elected as M.L.A. from 1983 onwards, on behalf of the T.D.P. from Sompet of Srikakulam district. Mr. G. Rajesham Goud has also been twice elected as M.L.A. and was also elected as Chairman of Zilla Parishad since 1994. He was a minister in Mr. N. T. Rama Rao cabinet. Mr. T. Devendar Goud who entered the T.D.P. became the Chairman of Zilla Parishad of Ranga Reddy district in 1988. He is also the polite-bureau member in the T.D.P. central committee. After winning the assembly elections as an M.L.A. in 1955, he joined as a minister for Backward Class Welfare and Prohibition in NTR cabinet. Subsequently he was appointed as a Minister for Revenue and Rehabilitation in Mr. Chandrababu Naidu cabinet. Smt. E. Seetharavamma was elected as M.L.A. from Kuchipudi of Guntur district. She was also appointed as a Minster for Women and Child Welfare in Chandra Babu cabinet. Mr. K.E. Prabhakar elected from Dhone constituency of Kurnool district in the by-election in 1996 and was appointed as a Minister for

Primary Education. Other important leaders belonging to the toddy tapper's community are Mr. Srinivasulu Goud Chairman, Zilla Parishad, Medak district, Mr. Kagithapu Venkata Rao M.L.A. and Mr. Gangadhar Goud who became the Chairman District Co-operative Bank at Nizambad.

A considerable number of Mandal presidents, Z.P.T.C., M.P.T.C and village Sarpanches have been elected on Maheshwaram Mandal of Ranga Reddy district, Smt. K.E. Jayamma Krishnagiri, Sanjannam Veldurthy, Bhuthpoor Mandal president etc. The candidates in the Telugu Desam party from the toddy tappers community are vastly different from those in the Congress Party. Firstly, are all relatively young. They are the sons of already established politicians or toddy contractors. In this sense they have not risen from the ranks as in the case of Congress party. It is Evident from the interviews that these belong to a new generation who would have no place in the Congress Party, which is already saturated with old timers. Further the interviews indicate clearly that the backward caste especially the toddy tappers was an important base of TDP. They are aggressive and have been able to get berth in the cabinet due to their economic clout and organisational ability. They also have base in the innumerable elected offices as member of the local bodies. Based on random interviews with several such member it is observed that the vote banks based on caste loyalties among the toddy tappers operates quite efficiently. The General Secretary of the Andhra Pradesh Toddy Tappers and Workers Federation and Mr. B. Prabhakar, who is also a member of Communist Party of India, has the toddy tappers as his support base.

Thus, while the community of toddy tappers were totally marginalised and had no say in the caste ridden traditional society, it is found that with intervention of election politics and democratic institutions, the members of this community have been integrated into the mainstream political process. Some members from the community have gained access to important electoral positions in the assembly and the Parliament. They have also risen to position of power. Their yearnings and aspirations to play an active role in politics have been satisfied by providing institutional framework such as the gram panchayats, mandal parishads and Zilla parishads, etc., at every level of decision making. They are among the most articulate leaders in electoral politics toddy.

Conclusion

In the fifty years history of the post-independent period, the toddy tappers movement has achieved some vital changes in the lives of the families. The political regime since independent thus gave scope for mobilisation of toddy tappers, who organised themselves to press for relief and by raising specific issues and demands. The government responded to these pressures and introduced welfare policies. Thus while it continued to depend on excise as a major source of revenue it did this with a 'human face'. The existence of the autonomous and independent political organisations of the toddy tappers generated a powerful political consciousness among them to become active participants in the ongoing political process. The electoral politics of the post-independent era had also contributed to the growing significance of toddy tappers as an important politics. This fact was very well recognised by them toddy as they aspired to become the representatives of the people. Some of the them became ministers.

REFERENCES

1. The Review of the state wide activities of the state committee (1957-81) released on the eve of the A.P. Toddy Tappers &

Workers Federation's 3rd state conference held at Vijayawada in 1982, p. 3.

2. Ibid, p. 3.
3. Biksham, B. Dharma. 1988. Geetha Karmika Sahakara Sanghalu upadiniche utpatichese kendraluga marali (the toddy tappers co-operative societies should be changed as centres of the employment and production) in Tapper (Savouneer. Hyderabad.
4. Goud. B. Adinarayana Murthy. 1993. Samagra Goudula Charithra, Sri Sarada publications, Bheemavaram (W. Godavari). P. 425.
5. Information is bases on interview with Mr. Dharambiksham Member of Parliament representing from Nalgonda constituency on behalf of Communist Party of Indian.
6. Ibid,.
7. The information on Mr. K.E. Madanna's rise in politics is based on interview with 1. Mr. K. E. Krishna Murthy, 2. Mr. Pullanna, 3. Mr. E. Ramanna Goud and 4. Mr. E. Ramesh.
8. Ibid.
9. He was the first Dalit Chief Minister of Andhra Pradesh.
10. The information is based on interview with Mr. Ramudu Journalist Eenadu 9Telugu Daily0 1996. Kurnool.
11. The information is based on interview with Mallikarjun Goud ex-central Minister and the president of the Andhra Pradesh Congress Committee.
12. Information is based on interview with Mr. T. Bala Goud ex-Member of Parliament representing from Nizambad constituency on behalf of Congress Party.
13. Goud, Adinarayana Murthy, 1993 the Profile of Political leaders of toddy tappers community in Samagra Goudula Charitra (A Comprehensive History of Goudus). Sree Sarada Publications, Bheemavaram (W. Godavari).
14. Ibid.

15. Ibid.

16. Ibid.

17. Ibid.

18. Ibid.

19. Venkatesu E. March 1996, Rathamaruthuna Geethannala Brathukulu (The changing lives of the toddy tappers) in Dalitarajyam (Telugu Monthly), Ponnur, Guntur.

20. Appala Swamy, Vangapandu, 1990, Sardar Gouth Lachanna (Biography), Sramika Riathanga Janavijanana pitam, Vishakhapatnam. P. 58.

21. Ibid. P. 515.

22. Goud, Adinarayana Murthy, 1993 The Profile of Political leaders of toddy tappers community in Samagra Goudulu Charitra (A Comprehensive History of Goudus). Sree Sarada Publications, Bheemavaram (W. Godavari).

23. Ainpur, L.S. Dynamic of Caste Relations in Rural India, Jaipur, Rawat Publications, 1986.

24. Gould, A. Harold. Hindu Caste System: the Socialisation of a Social Order, Delhi, Chanakya Publication, 1987.

25. Rao, V, Hanumantha. Party Politics in Andhra Pradesh 1956-1983, Hyderabad, ABA Publication, 1983.

26. Kothari, Rajani. Caste in Indian Politics, New Delhi, Orient Longman Ltd, 1970.

27. Syed Siraj Ul Hassan's, *"Caste and Tribes in Nizam Dominions"* Asian Educational Services, (reprient), Madras, pp. 240-241.

28. Thurston, E, *"Caste and Tribes of South India"*, (Vol.No.7) 1975. BAG, pp. 341-344.

29. Anthropological Survey of India's *'People of India (Andhra Pradesh)'*, Vol. No. XIII.

30. Chalamacharla Venkateshvarlu, *'Intaku Goudulevaru' (Telugu)*, Hyderabad, pp. 24 & 42.

31. Sir. N.E. Peale, in his writings *"Sugar Producing Palms"*.

32. *Dr. Buddiga Adinarayana Murthy's work 'Samgra Goudla Charita' (Telugu),* Sri Sharada Publications, Bhimavaram, 1993, p. 136.

33. Nargoni, V.G.R., *"Bharatha Desamlo Kallugitha Kulalu" (Telugu),* Secenderabad, 2002, pp.18-20.

34. Naa Jeevitam (Autobiography) in TELUGU written by *'Gouthu Latchanna',* 2001.

35. The ancient writer Col-Beber in his paper *'the Useful Plants of India',* (Asiatic Society in 1788).

36. Gudikadi Anjaneyulu Goud, *"Gouda Puranam Pattam Katha-Oka Parisilana"* (M.Phil).

37. Chendraiah, Medi, *'Gouda Settila Jevanaviddanam-Saeetyam'.*

38. Venkatesu, E., *'Excise Political-A Political Mobilization: A case study of Toddy Tapper in Andhra Pradesh',* unpublished M.Phil, University of Hyderabad, 1997, p. 28.

39. Appalaswamy, V, *'Sardar Gauthu Lachanna (Jeevitha Charitra) Biography of Sardar Gouth Lacchanna, Shramika Ryothanga-Janavignana-Peetam,* Vishakhapatnam, 1990, pp. 406-07.

40. Naragoni, V.G.R., *Rajakiya Antaranithanamlo B.C.lu* (Backward Classes in Political Untouchability), B.C. Garjana, February, 2000, pp. 36.

CHAPTER – 7

Baddam Yellareddy
A Biographical Study (1906-1978)

I Potanna

Introduction

Eminent Scottish historian Thomas carlyle that history is nothing but the biography of great men. And that it is a record of human a complishment particularly of great souls. A single virtuous a action of some one has many a time elevated a whole village, a whole city or whole nation to great name and fame.

Baddam yellareddy was core communist leader from nizam state during the free independent era. In this context I like to highlight the unique personality of telugu speaking area of erst while nizam state i.e., Baddam yellareddy. He was born in 1906 at karimnagar District, Siricilla thaluk, Galipalli village. His father was Hanmanth Reddy. Mother is laxmamma. He came from a middile class former family of peasants. His father was village "police patel". College education Vivekavardini school in Hyderabad. That time Nizam state under the control on (7th nizam) MIR OSMAN ALI KHAN.

During his young days he was deeply influenced the ideas and activities of eminent andra communist leaders

Yellareddy became influenced by the social ideas of Javaharlal Nehru. He belonged to the more militant sector in the Andhra

Mahasabha, that deplored the Non confrontational polices of the leadership of the organization. Baddam yellareddy influenced by Raavinarayanareddy, p. Sundarayya. Baddam yellareddy also participated in Non-cooperation movement in 1921 along with ravi narayanan reddy, gopal ravu ekbote, G.S. Melkote ,Baddam yellareddy went to Kakinada session of I.N.C in 1923. There he was along with his fellow senior leaders, he was arrested by police and sent to Ballary jail. There he came into contact with other communist revolutionary leaders. Baddam yellareddy was deeply in influenced by the Gandhian ideas and philosophy, after his release from jail, he returned to his village and started a school Harijan students he also propagated the use of khaddar cloth. According to him it was the symbol of Indian self respect, This tendency became increasingly attracted to communism in the late 1930's. Yellareddy took part in the 1938 Satyagrah. He was amongst those jailed during the protest compaign.In 1939 the communist parts of india established its organization in Hyderabad state, Baddam Yellareddy worked closely with Devulapally Venkateshwar Rao and Raavi narayana reddy in building Grassroot network of the party of the region.

The role of Baddam yellareddy in the activities of Andhra Mahasabha and the Telangana Peasants armed struggle

From 1941 Yellareddy's communist group came to dominate the Andhramahasabha, Yellareddy became the general secretary of the Andhramahasabha. Under Yellareddy's leadership the Andhramahasabha moved from being a liberal organization into a militant anti Nizam united front.

Yellareddy was one of the key leaders of the Telangana armed struggale. As the Nizam declared Hyderabad as an independent state in September 1947. Baddam Yellareddy was one of the signatories of a joint declareation of the communist party, Andhramahasabha and the all Hyderabad trade union congress. calling for armed struggle against the Nizam's rule and for the integration of Hyderabad in the Indian union (Yella Reddy signed on behalf of the Andhra Maha Sabha). The Telangana rebellion was one of the largest armed peasant uprising in modern India.

Baddam yellareddy's relations with kumaram bheem

Baddam yellareddy was a great supporter of tribal groups he extended his party's support to the heroic struggle of kumarram bheem the gond leader of Adilabad. He heard about Komaram bheem of Asifabad taluk in Adilabad District who fought against the tenannis of land lords. Asifabad taluk Sunkarpally village was his residence of Gonds.The land which was being cultivated by the Komaram Bheem was claimed by the landlord that landlord has the support of Thasildar, Girdawar, and police. Unable to do anything Bheem left that village and went to Sandhupur. He use to cultivate the land in the forest. One landlord named Siddiqui came and claimed that harvested crop was in his land Komaram Bheem lost the patience and people stood behind him. Police man fired on them. 10-12 Gonds members had died and some people of them were injured. Komaram Bheem escaped and police were searching for him.They were attacking on the people by listening that news. Yellareddy started to Asifabad. He visited the all villages and learn about the situation these details were printed in Golkonda news paper. Police have thought that he was encouraged the Gonds movement. C.I.D was being ordered to get the details of Yellareddy.

Police department sent report to the state Government on September 22,1940 as follows there were attempts of peasent struggle. There people of samsthan and two people belonging to the madras presidency were trying for this. Those two people of madras presidency were the leaders of communist - kisan movement. They were staying in state for the last 10 Months and spreading communist literature the details of these 5 persons were collected by the CID.

Political career and positions held by baddam yellareddy

Baddam Yellareddy served as secretary of the Telangana provincial committee of the communist party of India he was a member of the secretariat of the Vishalandra provincial committee of the C.P.I. In the first parliamentary elections held in 1951 after the emergence of Independent india yellareddy was elected to the loksabha in 1951 from karimnagar as a people Democratic Front candidate he defeated the congress party candidate PV Narasimha Rao (who later become the prime minister of India) In 1956 he become a control committee member of CPI. In 1958 he won a by election to the Andrapradesh Legislative Assembly from the Buggaram constituency.

The C.P.I party was splitted in 1964, Baddam yellareddy joined the Dissident Communist party of india (Marxist)Group. He was well prominent CPI leader in karimnagar District. Later he joined the C.P.I party.

Memorials

In 2006 in connection with yellareddy's birth centenary celebrations the AP chief minister of Andhra Pradesh Y.S. Rajashekar Reddy inaugurated a bronze statue of yellareddy in "karimnagar". At this ceremony the chief minister also vowed to realize the provision of additional "ayacut" through the completion of irrigation project in the karimnagar district, a dream project of yellareddy during his life time.

Conclusion

Baddam Yellareddy was one of the prominent leaders of Telangana who founded Andhra Mahasabha against Nizam's feudal system. He was the first person to support and stood for the upliftment of poor village people, he supported the against the opprasive rule British and landlords (Vetti chakiri). He was in front fight against British imperialism and Nizam Fuedalism. He supported the Telangana peasants he said " the cultivated land belongs cultivaters" he was the member of State Legislative Assembly appointed to study on the tribal's condition. The that took place on tribel of Srikakulam – Vijayanagaram – Vishakapatnam in the year 1977. As a committee member, he found that the money lenders of agency were looting the innocent tribals by collecting high rate of interest, unfortunately during the tour of agency he was attacked with paralysis pri treatment at Vishakapatnam he was rushed to Hyderabad finally his family moved him to his native village i.e Galipally. He died on 27th December 1978. The people of Karimnagar in particular and talagana region lost loveble leader Ravi Narayana Reddy shocked hearing the death news of martyr baddam yellareddy in radio, while he was in Bollipally. "The Great Star fall down, who beamed for the half dicades in the life style of telugu people". State government expressed its preference namely baddam Yellareddy as a district. In the past some districts named with the person names like Prakasham to ongole district, Konda Venkata ranga reddy to Rangareddy district. But naming the districts with the person name is not correct. Said by the Indian communist party and andhrapradesh state commity. CPI and Andhrapradesh state commity dicleared that naming the districts with the persons is not correct. But now communist party rejected that proposal of diclearing baddam yellareddy a district become of injustice. this decision spotlight become the during whether correct! or not? indian communist party show deep tribute to death of baddam yellareddy in salkiya of Bengal during the meeting 27th march in the year 1978.

REFERENCES

1. Ikeler, A.A (1972). Puritan temper and transcendentals faith. Carlyle's literary vision. Columbus, OH : ohio state university press.
2. Telangana pulibidda Baddam yellareddy. -kandimella prathap reddy.
3. Telangana people's struggle and its lessons. Sundaraiah. p
4. Report of the election commission of India Key highlights of General election 1951. (First Lok Sabha).
5. Project will changeface of karimnagar — The Hindu.
6. Official list of elected M.L.A to A.P. Assembly in 1972 report of E.C. 1972, P. 124.

CHAPTER – 8

A Dalit Prospective on Kakka Novel

NAGAJANU SUREPALLY

Introduction

The part of the poets and the anthologists to bring to light the Dalit ethos, angst, protest, heritage, myth and an alternative vision with a strong element of conscientising the Dalits and the non-Dalits including the oppressor. Some of the Dalit poets included in the anthologies were to become the most powerful voices in Dalit literature showing a direction to the young and emerging Dalit poets and literates. Jangam in Telangana region.

Folk beliefs in Post Independents

Once Ellaiah had visited Kalemma's house as usually (Kalemma is a kakka mother, Ellaiah is help for kakka lober work, some kind of only adviser in family). Agamaiah(he is kakka uncle) noticed him. He thought it's the right time to accuse them of having an illicit affair. Ellaiah called out Rammallaiah, and said, Look, my sister-in-law is a whore; what is going Kalemma with Ellaiah. Go and see it for yourself. He is very much in her house at the moment." and showed Ellaiah at Kalemma's house.' You being the chief of the caste, listen to me! We have to decide and settle the matter. Why is he visiting for her house?' Agamaiah brought the matter to the rachabanda, (village panchaity saba)stone-pedestal for the public resolution of the disputes. Rammallaiah, the chief of the caste, gave them a week's time setting the conditions, To settle what kind of a man he's, and what kind of a woman she's, each one has to choose four representatives for arbitrating the issue." that day. As the sun rose scorching, both of them deposited a thousand rupees each, and gathered at the tree of Mysamma, the folk-deity. Kalemma who didn't have a male-support, deposited her contribution of thousand rupees by selling a plate and a glass. Agamaiah and Ellaiah called for Kalemma to the rachabanda, where the caste folk assembled, Under this tree of ours – as Pochamma, the folk deity stands witness – tell us precisely what exactly had taken place. There should be nothing to hide. Rei, you caste folk, Agamaiah! You are the one who knows the fact; come to the fore, and tell us what had happened," they asked. Oyya, you the elders! I don't ever lie. Let me tell you the truth. Blinded by smugness, she's whoring herself to Ellaiah. She has lowered the status of our family; it's no sin even if she is killed. Having spread the end of her sari to sleep with Ellaiah, the wretch seems naive. If she claims that she is not sleeping with him, she should prove herself by swearing; she must place her hands in the cauldron of simmering oil; she should hold a blazing crowbar in her fists. Ask her if she agrees to these conditions," Agamaiah challenged. The representatives of Kalemma asked, Do you yourself agree to the conditions set by you?', I am ready for everything. If I do them all myself, would you get her head tonsured? Would you draw lime-designs on her scalp, and parade her in the streets seated on a black-donkey? (Meanest forms of punishment) She should be driven out of the village. Are you ready for the conditions? I swear by my wife and children. I swear by deity Muthalamma. I swear… Agamaiah poured a pot of cold water on himself making the atmosphere tense. The representative of Ellaiah got up to say, My client might be going to her house! Don't you ever go to anybody's house? Is that the reason why you had lived in the towns? Aren't we humans? Are we animals? How could one manage without ever going to others" houses? What has he done there, and how? Speak with conscience. We consider it a sin if at all we happen to witness the mating of the crows. Have you ever seen while they had met? Don't ever indulge in sinful talk; you will lose your eyes. Stop speaking lies! We are ready for anything if it's proved that our client is guilty.", Oho, is that so? Why does he visit the house of a lonely woman? What else do they have to do together? In that case, if I were to visit your house in your absence, will you ignore it?" Agamaiah questioned back. Aha, you are the one possessing a house in the village, and do you venture visiting my house ra? O.K, then; visit my house! Let me see how you would! I'll pierce you with a knife and garland you a wreath of cattle-meat. You whoreson!" the representative of Ellaiah fulminated. They had fisticuffs with each other. Agamaiah's dhoti and the banian were torn and soiled; the man seemed like a lump of clay. Having been humiliated, he said, Look, do you all understand now? You must tell me now. The caste folk are all one; they all plotted to kill me. She would certainly get me killed. Isn't she a whore? Aren't there men who carry the cot yearning for the can't, as the saying goes! Such a big altercation has taken place just because of an utterance; all of you can see it. Is it for nothing that he visits her, if it's not for sleeping with her?" Agamaiah dusted the soil off his clothes, and began to cry rubbing his eyes., Ei, stop for a while," another representative among them said. Standing up, he continued, What's the issue we have assembled here for? What's this awkward talk about? Do you keep quarrelling among yourselves without examining the tussle? Will you keep quiet or not?" Every one kept quiet. The dispute is not going to end this way but..." another representative intervened, Arey, O Irrigation-Eeraiah! Keep ready twigs of tamarind tree for beating her. She would speak out the facts only when thrashed. Is it going to be settled when we discuss the matter this way? Drag out that woman, Kalemma, ra. "Then, Irrigation-Eeraiah dragged Kalemma into the public by her hair. The representative of Ellaiah said, You must let us know if what all your brother-in-law had told us is true." Some of the elders spoke that Kalemma's not guilty. Rising up with pleading-hands, Kalemma said desperately, "Ayya, I am not guilty of any wrongdoing; why's it that I am harassed in this manner? I don't know anything about it. You have insulted me amid so many men; you have called me a raw-whore. I am not going to swear, since you all have insulted me and dragged me by hair. Then, the elders in the crowd discussed among themselves, What's this! How come she is speaking like that? She seems to have really slept with him. That's why Agamaiah might have planned for the public resolution of the dispute deliberately. An old man among the elders said, Let her sleep with him. But let's settle the matter by asking her to pay penalty for the offence she had committed. "Are we men or women? If we settle the matter this way, would any woman be scared of us in future? Keep quiet if you don't know!" they got irritated. They placed ready the canes of tamarind tree, a cauldron of simmering oil and a crowbar. Kalemma, who had noticed them all, got a wrench in her innards. She went to the heap of soil, and tossed it all over herself. She rolled around in the garbage, and behaved hysterically mad and foolish. She shouted, "Arey! You are all the men with a fistful of manly moustache, aren't you? A thousand rupees each that we have deposited is not meant for drinking toddy and liquor. O.K! You may drink! You are accusing me that I had slept with Ellaiah. If I really slept with him, does it shame you? You all have your wives and grownup daughters at home. Did they also sleep with him? Tell me if it's an insult to you. If anything, it's me, who is ashamed!" Kalemma screamed at the top of her voice. Getting up, Ellaiah said, Ehe, did I sleep with you? No, I didn't; I'm not of that sort. What's this, Kalemma?, Wait, you are anyway a man! Why are you worried? It's me who should be ashamed. Why do you worry? The, keep quiet!" Some of the elders pacified Ellaiah. My son is not young among the youth and not an elder among the grown ups; he's of eighteen years old. I swear by my lad. I'm not going to leave this village. Let me see how you're going to send me out of this village. Wasn't it in this village that my husband died; wasn't it here that he was buried? Wasn't it here that I had given birth to my lad?" Kalemma spoke out composed. Irrigation-Eeraiah whipped her on her back with canes of tamarind tree. Having developed cold sweat, Kalemma shivered, and urinated dripping past her legs. Irrigation-Eeraiah kicked on the bosom of Kakka, who tried to rescue his besieged mother. Kakka got tossed up, and fell down with a thud. They tied the lad with a damp rope as he was writhing in pain on the floor like a sacrificial goat at the deity of Mysamma. "Are you coming to shield your mother who shamed herself?" they called him names. Both the mother and the son stood thunderstruck being unable to speak as the caste folk uncoiled their talk against them. Though they knew it for sure the one who was in fact at wrong, the elders from each of the Madiga families looked at their face, spitting on them, Chi, wretchedness! When we seem nauseating to them all, why should we live in this village? We'll go somewhere from here," Kakka thought to himself. This is the village where Kakka's ancestors lived as members of the caste. Kakka continued to think to himself. If not this village, which we had considered our own till the death of the ayyamma, where else can we afford to live? Whichever village we might leave for, we may not have the Madiga entitlements. There may not be our rights among the caste folk near the Madiga-well. There's no question of leaving this village, why should we?" Kakka, who was deeply engrossed in these thoughts, was alerted when the chief of the Madigas spoke, "Arey, Irrigation-Eeraiah! Make a garland of sandals and marking-nuts, and hang it on the neem-tree in front of Kalemma's house; raise a fence of thorny-twigs around her house. Make a tom-tom with dappu, a drum in the surrounding villages that they have been excommunicated," commanded the chief.Having shaken hands with the elders, her brother-in-law, Agamaiah chased Kakka and Kalemma from the rachabanda to her hut. Then, they all pissed in a row around her house as a mark of insult. Having scolded them untiringly, everyone had left the place. The mother and the son entered into their hut, and closed the doors; they wailed and cried wildly. The house and the street seemed reverberated by their screaming, which sounded like a cyclonic wind.Kalemma thought, "The adversity of the kinfolk is so powerful. It's all just for not sleeping with my brother-in-law, a good-for-nothing fellow! He is so vengeful. My son has grown up enough to work as a field-labourer. Ehe, we can survive working hard somehow or the other. I'm a pure woman; if they label me a whore, do I become one?" thinking so, Kalemma fastened her chastity with a hearty hope. Yet, it's a life that's blamed. It pierced their heart having become a cactus. She's withered and singed having been greatly agitated. There's none to speak to her. No one offered her work in accordance with the caste-accord. "What am I going to do?" Kalamma endured a lot of persecution. She was not allowed access to the public water. She was not permitted to fetch fire for lighting her hearth. Her house was completely isolated from the Madiga-wada. All those coming from the neighbouring villages to attend weddings and functions labeled her house as the one belonging to a whore. "She is that kind of a woman; hence, a thorny-fence had been raised around her house," everyone commented. Wherever a few people gathered, Kalemma's episode became a big tale. His mother suffered so much just on account of deciding to stop her son from attending to the field-labour work. Her agony is un-narratable. She thought, "The grown up lad has been subjected to so much of humiliation right in front of my eyes." In the meantime, her son, about whom she's worried a lot, could become a senior field-labourer. „My son, who's detested by Papi Reddy patel, has now grown to be trustworthy to the same patel. Who knows about the steaming of a pot that's full to the brim? Just that very year, the fields yielded a wonderfully rich crop. The patel asked Kakka to process the grains, stuff it into the gunny bags, and get it by the bullock cart to the grain market in the town. Then, the patel left for the grain market early by his bicycle. The patel made a survey of the heaps of grains in the market finding out the price the government offered. Then he waited for Kakka looking in the direction of the track of the carts. The cart arrived. Kakka stopped the cart, and supported it with the wooden poles. He set off the bullocks, and tethered them placing some fodder in front of them.

Son was advice to Mother remarried lives

Writer is express humanism thing process, how it coming…social new ideological context. Every time he came to the grain market, Kakka befriended one Potter-Mangaiah who keeps selling pots at the market. Mangaiah, who noticed him, said, "Hei lad! You seem gloomy today. What s the matter? Kakka, who had always disclosed to him his pains and pleasures, began to narrate him in detail all that had happened. Kakka broke down holding his hands." The people are like crows, my lad. Since you are in trouble, I ll let you know something, do you oblige me? Hope you don t mind. You must assure me. "I swear by my mother; do I say no if you offer to lessen my sorrow?" You re a grown up man now; you can survive somehow. When someone offers you a bride, you would lead a conjugal life. I can understand the suffering of your mother in your village. Why don t you think of your mother, my lad? You re my dear one; don t think otherwise. There s a Madiga by name Bolguri Kondaiah in my village. He s young by age; he s the only son of parents. His parents died soon after his marriage. His wife died at the time of her first labour. He owns a wide courtyard. His life and caste-occupation are perfectly alright. Let me know your decision if only you would consent, my lad. Human beings endure suffering more than the cattle. We ll get him remarried. What do you say? Let me know, my lad! „What s this? You re speaking in such an awkward way! Ehe, keep quiet! You…, damn with your suggestion, agitated, Kakka. Having narrated to Kakka numerous problems and episodes, he said, "Keep pondering about your mother. Potter- Mangaiah narrated the problems that a single-woman would face in the society. He could convince Kakka at last by narrating the problems like knitting one bead after the other. Then, the patel who decided on the price of the grain shouted, "Arey Kakka! Unload the grain for the dealer; the price has been fixed ra. Kakka got alerted. Having handed over the bags of grain to the dealer, Kakka set the bullocks to the cart, and started for the village. Potter-Mangaiah hollered asking Kakka to think and decide on his suggestion." Fine, I ll come back to the market next Saturday taking permission from the patel. „Alright then, you may take leave, Potter-Mangaiah waved to him.He led the bullock cart back to the village. Having tethered the bullocks in the shed, Kakka went home by night. Soon after reaching home, he said, Mother, I am feeling hungry; serve me some food. She served him a plateful of food in haste, as her son had been out daylong. She served her son to his fill. Having eaten, he relaxed on the cot thinking, "whether to disclose the matter to her or, not? Kakka felt pained in his heart." Come what may, thinking so, he called out, "Amma, mother O amma! he addressed her so endearingly. Kalemma, who heard him call out, came out, and said "What s the matter, my son, what s the matter? she soothed the legs of her son, who got tired working the whole day." O amma, I ll say something; swear by me not to think otherwise. "What s it… what s it about?" Amma… when am I going to be married off? Why not my son? When we get a good bride, I ll certainly get you married off? Shouldn t we search for a girl matching our family? "That s what! I too desire the same as you are struggling all alone." Yes, that s right; I can toil to any extent for your sake. "Really so? Then for my sake, you must get married again, amma! You have to live with another man! You have to say yes, somehow." What s this, Kakka? Whoever might have told you this? Does the society spare us if one s son gets one s own mother married off? Arey, do you advise me to get married again? Kalemma thrashed him on his back with a worn-out broomstick.The neighbouring women of the village learnt about Kakka s proposal. They said one after the other, „If there s no man at home, you ll be blamed like this in future too. If a husband dies in our families, does the wife stay homebound? The bodily desires would surface one day or the other. You are anyway not old. The lad has grown up enough to cook his own food. Kalemma, you would face similar hardships if you don t have a husband. You have to but live with someone for your own sake. The near and the dear of the caste folk convinced her diligently. Even before his mother was awake, Kakka got up early in dark, and went on foot to the village of the new groom. Having gone to the house of Bolguri Kondaiah, Kakka took a look at the house and the surroundings. Then he went to Potter-Mangaiah, who proposed the match for his mother. Kakka said, "I ve seen the groom you had proposed. Everything is alright. I m convinced. You have to convince Bolguri Kondaiah. I ll arrange for the second-marriage of my mother to be performed on the next Thursday in the shrine of Muthalamma in my village. Kakka returned home from Potter-Mangaiah. Having washed his hands and feet at the water-trough, he went to the mother, and sat beside her. Kakka said, "Amma, I ve gone to the village where you would live after your remarriage. The man, Bolguri Kondaiah seemed a good man – the man who would be my father. He is excellent. He s not a man of anger. I m fixing your re-marriage precisely for what you had been humiliated. It should be like spitting with a clunk on the faces of all those who had humiliated you in the village! The following day was Thursday. She ground the millets on the grinding-slab, and cooked gatka with fermented-liquid that prevents staling. She mixed the gatka with onion, and fed her son handfuls. Mixing the rest of the gatka in water, she poured it into an earthen-pot, and placed it in the sling hanging to the roof-beam.Kalemma told her son, „Eat the gatka whenever you feel hungry, my son. You can have some of it tomorrow too. I m going to belong to someone else by next week. I ve to label myself with the surname of a fellow of another village. From a day after tomorrow onwards, keep cooking a small measure of rice, and eat. Don t worry about me, my son. Me? I ll look after myself very well. Let s go then. I ve brought the requirements of the marriage. Come; let s have a look at them. Betel nuts, dates, a sari, a shirt and a dhoti for father, blouse-pieces, waistcloth that forms a pouch, turmeric, kumkum and bangles – I brought them all. Let s go to the shrine of Muthalamma. Father has already arrived there. He bought toe-rings, bangles and pusthe, bridal neck-string. We have no one for us worth calling our own. They have all rejected us. No one is going to attend the wedding. You will not fall short of anything. When you put on all these, you would look like Yellamma, deity Renuka. Having accompanied his mother to the shrine, Kakka made Kondaiah knot the pusthe around his mother s neck. While sending off his mother and father from the shrine through the village, they wailed holding each other. Kakka asked his mother to take care of herself, and his mother in turn asked the son to take care of himself. "Amma, let me take leave of you, as the son said," Let me take leave of you, my son, the mother said. They consoled each other.Then, Kakka approached his stepfather, eyes streaming, and said, "Father, take care of my mother well. I ll keep visiting her now and then, he broke down irresistibly holding the hands of the father. Turning back, Kakka banged his head hitting himself on a stone." Why have you hit your head on the stone, my son? Having done so much for me, you have hurt your head; in that case I wouldn t go. "O, amma, don t worry. I couldn t stand the grief, and therefore I did so. Amma, you may please leave. Having kept hand in hand – the hands of the mother and the father – Kakka led them to the pathway of his mother s new in-law s village, and began to go home. The mother said while looking back," Ori Kakka, take care of yourself, my child. Kakka already walked too far to hear his mother s yelling.

"This fellow is so great! Being a son, he got his mother married off, the village folk felt it an unusual event. Looking at the people, Kakka was reminded of the humiliating incident of the tamarind-tree, canes, marking-nuts, and the blistered fingers that were dipped in the cauldron of simmering oil – the same hands that his mother reared him enduring so many hardships. He thought to himself, They had excommunicated my mother; accused her of being a whore; the people could say anything, but are they going to help us in troubled times? Kakka s eyes flooded. Having sent off his mother in the pathway of eyes, he thought, I m the one born the wrong side up, and such a man is damned to suffer. The caste folk don t belong to me; the mother left this village to lead a new life with another man. As she kept walking to her new in-law s village, she seemed like seams of clouds that move away in layered sheets. Kakka returned to his village from the outskirts; he reached home. The mother got remarried. He slept on a cot in the middle of the hut facing the roof. Then he looked at the sling hanging to the roof-beam. The knot of the bowl containing gatka seemed so cute. Mother s warmth is always like that. My mother, Kalemma should be happy always, thinking so; Kakka made the wick of the lamp smaller, and slipped into sleep.

Young life with historical ideology and culture

Kakka was started younger life with Pakirtaiah (tatha is village president, he knows madiga lid cap and historical ideology and culture), kakka need wants learning Madiga culture (Dappu, lid cap, Madiga culture dance it is called Chindu, Dakkali Baindla, Masti, Jambapuranam/Yaksaganam, Patam katha. Renuka Yallamma Katha) and bhagavata purana, whose name may be linked to "Chindu as a dancing step but is uncertain as to origin, had been the best known of the specialized performers in recent times. They have not only performed both the Gosangi Vesham explicitly for Madigas, and the Yellamma Vesham that goes with it but carries its relevance across caste boundaries, they have also in Telangana developed their own style of yakshaganam performance for a more general audience. The great stories mainly from the siva temple and Mahabharata that are widely popular in performance across Andhra Pradesh, had been acted out of in dialogue, song and dance, with musical accompaniment. These have been elaborately costumed performances with full make-up. The Dakkalis, formerly thought of as exclusively" beggars to the Madigas, had also promoted their own style of narration and acting. Kinnera is a stringed instrument played by Dakkalis as they recite the caste myth using scroll- narratives. Kakka should be happy always, his was leaning new ideology and culture. Pakirtatha and kakka were going with Dappu chatinpu surrounding villages. Kakka was lives at his Owen hut house sometimes sleeping with Pakirtatha hut house. lachakka lives with his grandfather (Pakirtatha), his had goats and bulls lachaka that going for bulls and goats, for security, grass and animals food and water daily work. Some times kakka also going. Kakka was working and learning under Pakirtatha teachings.

Kakka, when was he come younger age his had been wants a life partner (wife). But in village, every family was not interested to give girl. Madiga community was ideologically they want relation to elder families. Kakka was not younger surnames family, so his had been troubling. One day Pakirtatha was invited to Kakka in his house for dinner with vatithunakalu kurra (it s like a beef curry) .Kakka was visited Pakirtha house in their lachakka and tatha there. then tatha called to a-re kakka come and site here, lachakka was Food and beverage serving with little curry, tatha asked where is curry? She told to her tatha (grandfather). She wants to curry for Kakka. Kakka went out from tatha house to his house. Pakirtha was gone out to in their village. Lachakka visited Kakka house with vatithunakalu vepudu (beef fry), Kakka was questing to her, why was come my house this time? Her told to (Kakka) you don t know why am I come here? You had interested this curry, and we are not met since one week, aren't you forget our love?, are you searching another girl? Then kakka says, how possible forget your grateful love? you can love me, my dear lachakka. She was helped to kakka eating with love while Pakiratatha go to her house with listing their love issue. When she saw his tatha going sound, dark night, she was jumped from kakka house to her house.

Kakka was marriage; caste variations were beginning political way

Pakirtaiah, When he was sleeping, with further thing, she want husband so she is love to Kakka, how will arranged lachakka marriage, she lose mother and father, I am guardian of lachakka life. When will completed lachakka marriage, she is free living with her husband and family members. So I am very happy. Next day Kakka and tatha that going for security, grass and animals food and water of goats, bulls. Kakka, tatha I want madiga vata (sere, it s like drinking kallu vata and beef food, madiga surname sere during one year) Their pakirtatha was asked to Kakka ?a-re Kakka when will get the marriage ra emira aya Kakka when you gave papuannna (it s like a marriage dinner), Kakka told to tatha every one not give to girl, they want ballgame (it s like elder family and some sere) tatha you know what was my possession, then Pakirtha asked a-re Kakka you have interest marriage to Lachakka? Tatha why not? If you get the marriage come to join my family your surname changing (it s like elarikamm), then you will also getting vata (sere). Tatha but madiga caste and same your surname community may be they will not interest. And they were opposition to my marriage. Ok you don t thinking and don t worry about your marriage, I will arrange your marriage that was my responsibility ok na. Pakirtatha was proposal same elder surnames, their every family were opposition to Lachakka with Kakka marriage, they were said Kakka was lose his father in childhood , mother were remarried, his was lose house and many etc. If you arranged marriage and you help to Kakka live .We were should not come, we need to opposition his marriage culture. Pakirtatha and Kakka, they were going to side village for asking marriage details from Dakkali Muthaiah (he has been madiga astrology (it s like sating time of Muhurtham) Muthaiah fixed date and time, coming seven days good time. They were thinking how it s possible arranged marriage. Ok Kakka go to informed your side family members and I. Lachakka was clining hut and her thinking to house and earth decorating with red clay (it,,s called putamanu in Telugu). her and same women were gone to red clay place, every one taking red clay from same place .the place owner was come same time his name is Patel. he was arguing with dalit women s and he was ordering ,don t take red clay, why are saying wrong way this clay taking since Nizam's period. That time this land was my grandfathers. Every caste took form this place, so we want to red clay after two days Kakka weds Lachakka, I am saying don t took red clay ok na women s. You are not undressing my voice, madiga women (…it s like vulgar language) Pattel was slapped women s. one women fell down there with blood. They were knows issue, madiga community were complete to panchayati. They were called panchaity (rachabanda), women s rising voices to pattel. That time pakirtha was went out agadi for baka godu(not weaker animal) madiga community wants marriage things and beef food, they want good sodiffication….and not blamed food not well. While they were discussing about red clay issue he was joined that place all caste are took red clay, that time other caste are not supports to madigas. the arguing postponed next week (panchaithi vache varam lo jaruguthundi), due to pattel was completed to near their Kanchiamcerla Police station on madiga women s and madiga people. Marriage date was come Dakkali Muthaiah was coming for marriage working. When was marriage completed polices are visited madiga vada (street) Police says, Pattel was gave completed madiga community so and so names come to police station we are give Oder. After marriage madiga community from was pakiraiah go to Kanchiamcerla police satiation. He also had given complete on Pattel. Police was arrested madiga 4youngers and two elders (with Kakka also) after police were asking what was issue? Everyone not says in fort of Pattel. Next day Pakiraiah was visited police station while sub inspector was asking to Pakirtatha, what s happen that issue? He was says you don t knows sir; everyone is you knows because Pattel already informed to you sir. Pakirtatha you go to village I was released your community, and then next day Pakirtatha was not well he was died at night time in house. Madiga women s was informed to their kanchiamcerla police station for madiga community; the police was released madiga persons. They were running to village, there women s was crying and Lachakka. and Kakka was joined. After Pakirtatha karamlu was completed. after day Pattel called to vice president (Srinivas goud), president Pakirtatha was no more so you doing president, that issue going, one day madiga community discussing about village president leader by Kakka. We want president so become madiga community person. They were to go at Pattel house, they were asked questioned this time ruling my community so we want preside ship, ama-aera kakka yours asking to me and questioning? no, it's not possible next president may be will Srinivas goud. Then they return to houses. Celebrating rally for new presidential election with bull cat pattel in village. Pattel was main role. But ruling and very thing doing Pattel, but president was Srinivas goud. One day Kakka and his friend goes to kallu drinking for they vata (sere) that time Srinivas goud meet to kakka. kakka asked to Srinivas goud do you know pattel knowledge you was president but ruling and very thing was doing pattel. Yours and my community lose the president ship. Kakka was drunken back to his house lachakakka was waiting for kakka. He was enter the house suddenly lachakka went out back side of house she draw on house hall tree lines with bogu (balck gold). Kakka was asking what happen to lachakka? Her told this is third month.(pregnant women), lachakka and kakka were sitting in house lachakka you are sing song very well I know an kamudu festival day.

Conclusion

These features are characteristic of orality. Sindu Yakshagaanam, the most popular form of the Dalit folk art; the art of the Dakkali s who recount the family-lineages of the Madigas; the manner of the speech of an illiterate Dalit in the day-to-day communication have a perceivable influence in the narration of Kakka. The avoidance of the punctuation allows the flow of narration in the manner of Dalit Street-plays. The use of the work-chants/songs, songs of various rites, festivals, bonfires and the songs from the street plays is characteristic of the Dalit forms of fork arts. Other features of Dalit folklore include the use of proverbs and abuses that Kakka abounds. May not be out of place. The abuses are the most intrinsic part of the conversation of the illiterate Dalit men and women. But what is noteworthy is that the Dalits use the abuses without meaning or intending the pejorative sense of the abuses. Yellaiah uses the abuses in the novel true to the conversation of the Dalits in real life.The second linguistic distinctiveness is the use of the Telangana dialect, which is employed not only for the dialogue but also for the narrative. However, it is not a new experiment to write a novel in the Telangana dialect. Other writers who successfully experimented with the dialect for fiction include Thummeti Raghothama Reddy and Allam Rajaiah in the Telangana dialect, Chakaravenu and Namini Subrahmanyam Nayudu in the Rayalaseema dialect and Raavi Saastri in the coastal dialect. In Kakka, Yellaiah goes ahead of these writers by using the Telangana dialect as spoken by the rural illiterate Dalits.Finally, Yellaiah complements the oral tradition and the Telangana dialect with the Madiga register. On this count, Kakka is the first of its kind as far as Telugu Dalit literature is concerned. What the novelist achieves by means of this is that the readers get an original feeling of what Dalit language is like. The portrayal of incidents dealing with the Madiga occupations such as processing bullock-hide, making leather goods, playing on the drum, rendering agricultural services; cultural aspects like the rituals of birth, death, wedding, puberty, eating bullock-meat and so on are rendered using their own register, as the incidents portrayed are culture specific; Madiga specific.To express it in the stylized, standard, neutral Telugu would have been at the cost of the essential Dalitness. Neutral expressions would generally convey positive connotations romanticizing the Dalit experience. Yellaiah Anna (brother) avoided the neutrality of expressions successfully by employing the socialist of the Madigas. In effect, Yellaiah s attempt at reclaiming the Dalit language by means of linguistic distinctiveness is aimed at Dalitising Telugu language by liberating it from the influence of Sanskrit as well as the written Telugu. The caste hierarchy and inter-personal relations among the people of various castes is communicated, and best understood by the inflections suffixed to the names and pronouns of the Dalits by the upper caste men. Morphs such as, arey, vay, ra and various forms of abuses and scolding are rendered in English to convey the sense of social hierarchy in the caste system. The belief that all behavior, opinions, etc. Their understanding of discrimination, exploitation, disputes, protest and rebellion, which are germane to the Madiga Others. The social, economic and political subalternity is treated with the symbols of Madiganess. Yellaiah chooses a suitable form to represent the Dalit life In Kakka.

REFERENCES

1. Vemula Ellaiah: kakka (dalit novel), Gosangi (Neeli Sahithi), Nalgonda, publishes-04, June-2000.
2. Dr. Pulikonda Subbachary, Telugulo Kulapuranalu-Asrita Vyavastha (A Study of Caste Myths and Dependent, Caste System of Telugu) Publishes: Prajashakti Daily Printing Press Hyderabad, May-2000.
3. Interviewing: Vemula Ellaiah about Kakka (dalit novel) and his personal ideas.

CHAPTER – 9

Scheduled Tribes Education Development in Khammam District: An Analytical Study

E. SOMLA NAIK

Introduction

Education is a fundamental right of all citizens. The fifth Constitutional amendment Act has made primary education as a fundamental right to the children of 6 to 14 years of age. The Government of India and the State Government are taken steps to fulfil this right. It is a fact that education is an essential programme for economic growth and development of the society and it is an investment and a human capital. It enhances individual's well being. Literacy is proved to be a key variable for the development of the society and success of democracy. Illiterate people tend to have low self-esteem and low social stats. Because of their illiteracy they cannot reap the fruits of democracy. Education is of value not only for the person who acquires it, but also for others. Widespread of education helps to resolve social problem like poverty, ignorance, illiteracy, diseases, population growth and environmental degradation[1]. To march towards bright future the only hope rests with educational persons. Mahatma Gandhi was of the opinion that education is the basic tool for the development of consciousness and reconstruction of the society. In India both the Scheduled Caste and Scheduled Tribes were had very low literacy rate. The government of India provided certain facilities for the development of the Scheduled Caste and Scheduled Tribes education in the country. But the government effort should not impact on the both the Scheduled Caste and Scheduled Tribes Education. In Telangana State, the government has neglecting the Public Education. Particularly Scheduled Caste and Scheduled Tribe budget is diverting other developmental activities in the State. Most of the Scheduled Tribes were dropped their education in the middle of the academic year due to lack of poverty.

District

Khammam is one of an important district in Telangana State. Its name derived from Khammamet, which in turn appears to have derived it, form a hill known as the Stambhadri located in the heart of the town. As the pillars (Stambhams) capable of supporting the ceiling of temples and Mantapas could be made of the tall stones of the hill, the town was termed variously as Stambhadri, Stambhagiri, Khambagiri and Khammamet, the last of which being a Telugu version of Stambhagiri[2]. The District located between 16° 45' and 18° 35' north latitudes and between 79° 47' and 80° 47' east longitudes. It is bounded on the north by Madhya Pradesh and Orissa States, on the south and east by Andhra Pradesh State and west by Nalgonda and Warangal District respectively.

Area

Telangana is one of the biggest State in Southern Region and it was a new State in the Indian Union emerged as 29th State according to the Andhra Pradesh Reorganisation Act, 2014 of Parliament, which received the assent of the President of India on the 1st March, 2014 and came into the existence with effect from 2nd June, 2014 with the city Hyderabad as its capital. In the State there are 10 Districts such as Adilabad, Karimnagar, Warangal, Nizamabad, Medak, Rangareddy, Hyderabad, Mahaboobnagar, Nalgonda and Khammam[3]. But in 2016 the Telangana State was announced several new Districts including the old Districts. Now the total Districts in the state are 31. Our paper is focus only on the old Khammam District. The District was the 4th largest District in Telangana State according to geographical area. The District total area is as follows:

Table 1

Geographical area of the Districts (in Sq.Kms)

Sl. No	*District*	*Geographical area*
1.	Adilabad	16,105
2.	Nizamabad	7,956
3.	Karimnagar	11,823
4.	Warangal	12,846
5.	Nalgonda	14,240
6.	Khammam	13,266
7.	Mahaboobnagar	18,432
8.	Rangareddy	7,493
9.	Hyderabad	217
10.	Medak	9,699

Source: Statistical Year Book, 2016, Directorate of Economics and Statistics, Government of Telangana, Hyderabad, P. 13.

The above table 1 reveals that the one of the biggest District in Telangana is Khammam its place is 4th. The first three biggest Districts are Mahaboobnagar, Adilabad and Nalgonda. Hyderabad is the smallest District in Telangana State. Khammam is the one of the backward region in the state. But it had rich mineral resources. The District was border between the Telangana and Andhra Pradesh. The District played a vital role in the Telangana State development. In the District major population is scheduled tribes. They were backward in terms of education and economy.

Population

Tribal population of the Telangana State, according to 2011 Census, is 32.87 lakhs which constitutes 9.34 percent of the total population of the State. ST literacy rate is 49.51 as against State literacy rate of 66.46. There are 32 Tribal groups living in the State which include 4 PvTGs (Particularly vulnerable Tribal Groups – earlier known as Primitive Tribal Group) viz., Kondareddies, Chenchus, Kolams, Gond and Thoties[4] living in Khammam, Mahaboobnagar, Nalgonda, Ranga Reddy, Adilabad Districts. The dominant tribal groups in the State are Lambada with a population of 20,46,117, Koyas – 4,86,391, Gonds – 2,97,846, Yerukalas – 1,44,128. In Khammam District the tribal's are Koyas 1,50,209[5] in this males are 75,114 and females are 75,095 Gonds were 14,858, males are 7,351 and females are 7,507 are very important communities in 1961 in the District. Later the Lambada community occupied prominent place in the District. According to ITDA information the Lambadas are 3.29 lakhs, Koya 3.14 lakhs, Yerukala 0.20 lakhs, Konda Reddi 0.10 lakhs, Yanadi 0.07 lakhs and other Scheduled Tribes are 0.03 lakhs. The Government have accorded high priority for accelerated development of Tribals by implementing socio-economic development schemes. The major focus is on Education, Economic support and land based schemes. The details of the tribal population in the District as follows:

Table 2
Khammam District population

Category	*Male*	*Female*	*Total*
General	12,98,543	13,08,523	26,07,066
Scheduled Caste	2,18,100	2,20,916	4,39,016
Scheduled Tribe	3,26,225	3,30,352	6,56,577

Source: Statistical Year Book, 2015, Directorate of Economics and Statistics, Government of Telangana, Hyderabad, PP. 28-29.

The above table reveals that the total population in Khammam District and Scheduled Tribe population both the male and female respectively. Scheduled Tribe male population is 3,26,225 and female population is 3,30,352. Female population is more compare with the male population not only Scheduled Tribes but also General population in the District. Total population is 26,07,066, the Scheduled tribes are 6,56,577[6] and scheduled Castes are 4,39,016 respectively. Both the Scheduled Tribes and Scheduled castes occupied 50 percent in the total population. But they are very backward in terms of education and economical weak.

Educational Institutions

The Government of India with an objective to provide universal education to all of its citizens has enacted the Right of Children to Free and Compulsory Education Act, 2009 to provide for Free and Compulsory Education to all the children in the age group of 6 to 14 years, in the country. In order to achieve this objective, need exists for ensuring access to education, gender parity in school enrolment, overall enrolment and retention and the quality of education being imparted. In the light of Right of Children to Free and Compulsory Education Act, 2009, the Government has taken various initiatives for universalization of elementary education like strengthening of existing schools, opening of new primary schools, and other type of educational facilities in remote and un-served habitations, in the State and in the District. There are 43,293 schools functioning under various managements during 2013-14 in the State, imparting quality education to pupil. The students enrolled during the year are 61.78 lakh, consisting of 31.59 lakh boys and 30.19 girls. The teachers deployed are 2.35 lakh and the teacher-pupil ratio is 26.

In Khammam District the Government schools were 484, in this the boys 9,057, girls 8,917 and the total strength is 17,974. MPP and ZPP schools were 1,918, in this the boys strength is 44,091, girls 45,339 and the total strength is 89,430. Aided schools were 47, in this the boys 3,799, girls 4,328 and the total strength is 8,127 and the un-aided schools were 223, in this the boys 26,683, girls 20,756 and the total strength is 47,439. The total schools in the district is 2,672, in this the boys are 83,630, girls 79,340 and the total strength is 1,62,970[7]. The teachers strength is 7,142, in this male teachers are 3,769 and female teachers are 3,373 respectively.

Enrolment

In Khammam District the Scheduled Tribes enrolment in the Primary schools are very low compare with other communities in the District. . Scheduled tribes literacy rate and enrolment is very less and their dropout is more in the District. The enrolment of the Scheduled Tribe children from 1st to 7th class from 2001 to 2007 details as follows.

Table 3
Enrolment of Children in different classes in the District

Year	*Class*	*Total of all Castes*	*Scheduled Caste*
2001-02	1	63,658	27,390
	2	59,485	23,659

contd. table 3

Year	*Class*	*Total of all Castes*	*Scheduled Caste*
	3	62,280	23,235
	4	55,989	17,901
	5	47,559	12,912
	6	40,449	9,794
	7	31,600	7,076
2002-03	1	61,296	12,788
	2	57,875	11,719
	3	59,350	11,519
	4	59,638	10,199
	5	57,392	7,958
	6	46,829	5,353
	7	38,645	3834
2003-04	1	51,924	20,490
	2	54,661	21,302
	3	54,791	21,680
	4	54,545	20,880
	5	56,832	19,746
	6	50,968	15,503
	7	42,047	11,465
2004-05	1	47,770	17,977
	2	45,632	16,517
	3	50,851	19,033
	4	52,230	19,647
	5	54,231	19,772
	6	53,303	17,708
	7	47,547	14,015
2005-06	1	53,891	20,351
	2	44,106	15,525
	3	45,119	15,876
	4	48,912	17,486

contd. table 3

Year	*Class*	*Total of all Castes*	*Scheduled Caste*
	5	51,459	18,064
	6	50,198	17,166
	7	49,578	15,956
2006-07	1	55,990	20,576
	2	48,741	17,264
	3	44,374	15,196
	4	44,585	14,872
	5	49,175	16,755
	6	49,819	16,484
	7	47,112	15,286

Source: Adinarayana Reddy.P, Uma Devi,D & Mahadeva Reddy.E: Tribal Education, Problems and Strategies, Sonali Publications, New Delhi, 2010, PP. 46-48.

The above table reveal that the total Scheduled Tribe student strength is decreased year by year in every class. In 2001-02 the Scheduled Tribe enrolment in the 1st class is 27,390 and in 2006-07 the enrolment of the caste is 20,576 respectively. The growth rate is increased every year in developing countries in different sector but in education sector particularly Scheduled Caste and Scheduled Tribe enrolment is decreased. At the same time in second class the enrolment of the Scheduled Tribe is 23,659 and in 2006-07 are 17,264[8]. From 1st to 7th class the gross enrolment of the particular community in Khammam District is deceased year by year due to lack of the government interest on education sector. Not only the Scheduled Tribes but also other community children enrolment is also very poor in the District.

Dropout Rate

In India 29.6 percent of the Scheduled Tribe population in the age group of 7 years and above is found to be literate as per the

1991 census; the literacy rate being 40.65 for males and 18.19 for females. These figures are much lower than the corresponding figures for the total population of India. In fact these figures are even lower than the corresponding figures for the Scheduled Caste population. If we were to take out the population of north-eastern States like Nagaland, Mizoram, Meghalaya and Manipur which have predominantly Scheduled Tribe population[9] and very high literacy rates, the literacy rate of the Scheduled Tribe population would become much lower. That is, the literacy levels among Scheduled Tribe population in other State are extremely low. In Andhra Pradesh particularly Khammam District literacy rate of the Scheduled Tribe population was 37.87 percent. In Khammam District the Scheduled Tribe children dropout rate is more compare with the statistics. The dropout of the children from 1st to 7th is 76.8 percent in this the boys dropout rate is 74.27 and girls dropout rate is 79.97 in 2001-02. In 2002-03 the boys dropout rate is 68.53, girls dropout rate is 73.9 and total dropout rate is 70.95, in 2003-04 boys dropout rate is 59.55 and girls rate is 61.86 and total dropout rate is 60.61[10], in 2004-05 boys dropout rate is 55.59 and girls dropout rate is 57.61 and total dropout rate is 56.56, in 2005-06 boys dropout rate is 61.62 and girls dropout rate is 66.6 and total dropout rate is 64.09 and in 2006-07 boys dropout rate is 43.24 and girls dropout rate is 48.93 and total dropout rate is 46.12 respectively.

The main causes for the dropout is poverty of the parents, contents of education, inadequate educational institutions and supporting services, absenteeism, Medium of instruction and government Education policy etc. due to the parent poverty most of the children were far away from the education. The scheduled Tribes below poverty line in 1977-78 is 72.4, in 1983-84 58.4 and in 1987-88 is 52.6 percent[11] in India respectively. In

Khammam District above 60 are under the below poverty. The general contents of education have been extended to the tribal areas which in many cases are not relevant, particularly at the primary stage. The tribal areas suffer from inadequacy of educational institutions, boarding and lodging facilities. Even where centres have been opened, about 40 percent of them are without buildings. The supporting services, such as the incentives in terms of scholarships, book banks, etc are very insignificant and generally do not attract the children. In the tribal areas the problem of absenteeism of the teachers is one of the basic important factors affecting the education. They generally remain absent for days together due to absence of supervision over them and also due to lack of dedication to the cause of education of the tribals[12]. The children and also the parents cannot afford to waste their time and generally opt to drop out from the schools. For the tribals the medium of instruction in the schools is a difficult problem. Even 60 years of independence we have not been able to provide education to the tribals in their mother tongue[13]. The tribal children are not generally able to follow the lessons given to them in the school in the language which is totally strange to them.

Welfare Hostels

Government has taken several steps for the growth of education in the State. It has been taking numerous welfare measures for importing quality education to all those children whose parents are not in a position to offer education to their children by establishing residential schools and hostels in the State. There are 780 hostels with a strength of 61,526 students for scheduled Castes, 203 hostels with a strength of 43,361 students and 283 ashram schools with a strength of 84,558 students for scheduled tribes and 737 hostels with a strength of 58,428 students for backward classes welfare functioning in the State during 2014-2015. Particularly in Khammam District Residential hostels were 45 in this boys strength is 5,503 and girls strength is 3,189 and total strength is 8,623. At the same time the ashram schools are 76 in this the boys strength is 11,849 and girls strength is 14,891 and total strength is 26,740. Adilabad and Khammam Districts occupied first and second place in the number of ashram schools and total strength of the students. In Khammam District number of the Social Welfare schools is 13 and tribal welfare schools are only 6. These figures show the Government interest on the Tribal education development in the State and also in the District. Due to the Government negligence most of the Tribal students and the scheduled Castes students were interest on education. There is unemployment also cause for the dropout of the students. According to 2016 Statistical Year book, the Scheduled Tribe literacy rate in Khammam in 2011 is 51.59 in this male literacy rate is 59.75 and female literacy rate is 43.67.

Conclusion

In Telangana State the Tribal community is very backward in terms of Socio-economic and education. Modern Government indirectly encouraged the Private sector and also Private Educational institutions. Most of the people are even now very backward and below the poverty line in the State. They prefer Government Institutions and Government Schools even today in different parts of the State. Their children also interest for Government Education. Lack of the government interest on education most of the students are not known the education and they are engaged as car drivers, labour, agricultural workers and factory worker in the different town in the State. The government also diverted scheduled Caste and Scheduled Tribe educational funds for other developmental works in the State.

There is contractual system is prevailed in the education sector and they were not trained and they don't know the tribal dialect and they are un-able to teach the tribal kids in the primary sections. At the same time teachers absenteeism is also led for the dropout of the Scheduled Tribe Students in the State and also in the country. The community demanding for establish more welfare hostels and residential schools to the students in the State. They were also demanding for special funds for the development of tribal education in the State.

NOTES

1. Midatala Rani: Problems of Tribal Education in India, Issues and Prospects, Kanishka Publishers & Distributors, New Delhi, 2009, P.1.
2. Raja Gopal, M.V: Andhra Pradesh District Gazetteers, Khammam, The Government Central Press, Hyderabad, 1977, P. 1.
3. Statistical Year Book, 2016, Directorate of Economics and Statistics, Government of Telangana, Hyderabad, P.13
4. Report of the Scheduled Areas and Scheduled Tribes Commission, Government of India, Vol-II, 2002-2004.
5. Raja Gopal, M.V: Andhra Pradesh District Gazetteers, Khammam, Op-Cit, P. 208.
6. Statistical Year Book, 2015, Directorate of Economics and Statistics, Government of Telangana, Hyderabad, PP. 28-29.
7. Statistical Year Book, 2015, Directorate of Economics and Statistics, Op-Cit, P. 266.
8. Adinarayana Reddy.P, Uma Devi,D & Mahadeva Reddy.E: Tribal Education, Problems and Strategies, Sonali Publications, New Delhi, 2010, PP. 46-48.
9. Amar Kumar Singh and Jabbi, M.K: Status of Tribals in India, Har-Anand Publications, New Delhi, 1996,P.16.

10. Adinarayana Reddy.P, Uma Devi,D & Mahadeva Reddy.E: Tribal Education, Problems and Strategies, Op-Cit, PP. 50-51.

11. Singh, A.K: Tribes and Tribal life, Sarup & Sons, New Delhi, 1993, P. 34.

12. Verma, R.C: Indian Tribes, through the Ages, Publication Division, Government of India, New Delhi, 2002, P. 104.

13. Midatala Rani: Problems of Tribal Education in India, Issues and Prospects, Op-Cit, P. 11.

CHAPTER – 10

Art and Culture in Telangana : A Historical Study

Marupu Venkatesham & Nagajanu Surepally

Introduction

Telangana Art & Culture If we see Andhra Pradesh consists of three distinct regions now separate state of telanagana), namely, Andhra, Rayalaseema and Talangana. Andhra and Rayalaseema were part of Madras province of the British Empire. For approximately 400 years, Telangana was part of Hyderabad State, an independent kingdom ruled by Muslim Qutub Shahi and Nizam dynasties. The history of Telengana began with the spread of Aryan civilization into this region. Early settlements in this region according to Buddhist works were along the banks of river Godavari in continuation with Muliki around Paithan in Aurangabad district of Maharashtra and Asmaka with Podana or Bodan as capital. Bodan was a sacred place according to Jaina literature. There were many local chieftains or kings in this region in the historic period and they came under the rule of Mauryan Empire. It is only after Ashoka the concept of sovereignty came to be known in this area. Ashoka introduced a highly organized system of administration based on the concept of central authority. It took two more centuries for Telugu people to unite under the leadership of Chimuka the first ruler of Satavahana dynasty. The first major dynasty to rule the region was the Shathavahana. Before the Shathavahana, there were many local rulers in different parts of Telengana such as Gobada, Narana, Kamvayasa, Sirivayasa and Samagopa. Samagopa ruled a large area for very long time. He issued a variety of coins of different denominations and in different metals. His rule was followed by that of Chimuka and coins with counter struck marks confirm this fact. All these local kings ruled from Kotalingala and early rulers of the Shathavahana dynasty also ruled from here. The Shathavahana rule commenced around 30 BC and it spread far wide. There were great kings like Satakarni I, Pulumavi-I, Hala, Gautamiputra Satakarni, Yajana Satakarni etc.who by virtue of their political conquests, efforts to promote trade and commerce and patronage of arts left a rich legacy of their rule. It was during this period, the famous Buddhist stupas at Amaravati, Battiprolu, Gudivada, Pedda Ganjam, Dhulikatta, Kondapur in Andhra and cave temples at Karla, Nasik, in the Maharastra and great stupa at Sanchi in Malva were built. The rule is believed to have received royal patronage from Yajana Satakarni. The Satavahana rule ended in 230 AD. The large number of Satavahana coins found in various parts of Decan bear testimony to the enormous trade activity during their period. This includes trade with Roman Empire in the beginning of Christian era, which earned large quantities of gold in exchange for cotton, pepper, ivory, aromatics and precious stones. It is interesting to recall that Magavahana dynasty ruled north coastal Andhra when Satavahasnas were ruling Telengana and Vidarba.

Telangana is situated on the central stretch of the Indian Peninsula, most of it on the high Deccan Plateau between the Aryan North and Dravidian South. The earliest mention of this region is to be found in the Aitareyabrahmana. It figured subsequently in the Ramayana and Mahabharatha and in the Puranas. It became "the region eminently suited for the fusion of the two cultures". The language of the people was Dravidian, called Telinga. The race and language had a glorious history that spans over 1000 years. The people had distinct style of their own in the fields of literature, music, dance, painting and sculpture. This culture acted as a bridge between the North and South. There were many Buddhist monasteries built in this region.

The Evolution of Festivals

Festivals are celebrated with much fervor and people used to go to temples on these days to offer special prayers. Festivals are listed below. Ugadi, Guru Purnima, Sri Rama Navami, Hanumajjayanti, Raakhi Pournami, Vinayaka Chaviti, Dusserah, Nagula Chaviti, Krishnashtami, Deepavali, Mukkoti Ekadasi, Karthika Purnima.

Folk art forms and their significance

The study of folk literature is essential to understand the life and philosophy of the rural masses who constitute the great majority of Indian population. The beauty of their hearts, their longings and aspirations and their beliefs and convictions are codified in the folk tales, legends, songs and stories. This oral literature embodies the hoary wisdom accumulated over hundreds and thousands of years. For the simple villagers throatier provides active social and spiritual guidance, offers a practical philosophy of life, and sets before them models and ideals for emulation. Telangana, which consists of the ten northern districts of Andhra Pradesh, is very rich in speech genres and folk narrative traditions. Prior to Independence, for various historical reasons, the people of Telangana led a secluded life which resulted in the evolution of a distinct folk culture of their own. This region has not gone through the same phases of cultural transformation as the rest of Andhra Pradesh. Even to this day there is a touch of primitive freshness about life in telangana. Added to this, a relative lack of individualism, strong community bonds and the unselfconscious, spontaneous and emotional nature of the people have contributed a great deal to the growth of the folk arts including the narrative arts. Often sentiments like great good fortune reaching the audience or the patrons are attached to the performance of these arts. Thus even superstition played a role in nurturing them. Until the radio, films, and more importantly the TV encroached upon their territory, the folk narrative and performing arts were the only source of collective entertainment and education for the villagers. There was also the leisure and willingness on the part of the villagers to patronize, appreciate and benefit from these arts. Most of these narrative art forms are traditionally practiced by certain marginalized sub-caste groups who depend on the dominant communities for survival. Some of these important narrative communities are: Addamsingvallu, Veedhi Bhagavatulu, Budige Jangaalu, Chinduvallu, Dasarivallu, Ganjikootivallu, Gollasuddulavallu, Gondaleelu, Jangaalu, Kakipadigelavallu, Koonapulivallu, Maladasarulu, Mandechulu, Matlevallu, Oggulu, Pichukakuntlu, Pondavulavallu, and Sharadagallu. Apart from these, there are also the non-caste specific teams such as batukamma teams, burrakatha teams, kolatam teams, and yakshganam teams. Depending on their traditional training the performance patterns and methods of presentation vary a great deal.

A Compendium of Tales, Legends & Stories

Some of the tales, legends and stories listed below are derived from the Ramayana, the Mahabharata and other all India epics and Puranas but they are often characterized by a significant variation on the original stories. Some are pure extensions of the epic and puranic tales. According to an estimate there are also at least thirty caste-specific Puranas in Telangana. The origin of these Puranas and non-derivative narratives is difficult to trace but it may be conjectured that they originated in the prehistoric past and have been transmitted orally from generation to generation, mainly through the medium of the narrative communities. There are also legends describing the glory and valour of local heroes and village deities as do those of the presiding deities of certain temples where fairs are held annually. Chirutala, yaksha (yakshaganam), oggu, natakam, and Jangam (mentioned in parentheses against some of the following entries) denote the main narrative modes of those particular stories.

Telangan it is not only celebrate the main festivals, but also celebrate certain regional festivals like Bonalu in Hyderabad, Batakamma all over Telangana districts, Yedupayala Jatara in Medak, Sammakka Saralamma in Warangal district. Other festivals are Nomulu Vrathalu Kedareswara Vratam , Madana Dwadasi Vratam, Vinayaka Vratam, Saraswati Vratam, Varalakshmi Vratam, Krishanshtami Vratam,Ananta Padmanabha Vratam, Margasira Lakshmi Varapu Nomu Katha, Polala Amavasya Vratam, Kumkuma Gowri Nomu,Sraavana Mangalavara Nomu Katha, and Karthika Deepala Nomu. A large majority of these tales and legends are not available in recorded form-written, taped or filmed-and therefore the need to record, compile and preserve them before they are lost forever. Sammakka Sarakka Jatara, also known as Medaram Jatara, is the magnificent fair celebrations in Telagana region of Andhra Pradesh. It is the second largest religious congregation after the Maha Kumbh Mela with about 7 million pilgrims attending the jatara. This jatara is held once in two years at Medaram village located at about 110 km from Warangal city, Warangal district of Andhra Pradesh. The jatara is held for three days before Magha Purnima January-February). In the year, jatara starts on 27th January and ends on 30th January.

Sammkka Sarakka Jathara

This Jatara celebration by the tribal people of Tadvai mandal, Medaram (vil), in Prof. Jayashankar Bhopalpally District. Medaraju was a contemporary of the Kakatiya king Rudradeva. He ruled polavasa kingdom. His daughter sammakka marriage with Pagidigiddaraju. He ruled medaram region. He had three children called Saralamma, Nagulamma, Jampanna. Pagidigiddaraju not paid the tax to Kakatiya rulers because severe famines for four years. Prataparudra – I declared the war on Medaram region. Pagidigiddaraju entire family bravely fight against the Kakatiya's army. All of them got killed in the battle. Jampanna also fought bravely till his last breath and died in "Sampanga Vagu. Sampangavagu now called Jampanna Vaagu. The people celebrate the Medarama Jatara. The Medaram Jatara is organized once in two years. It is three day fair. The people offer Bangaram Jaggery to the goddesses

Festivals

Batukamma Festival

The months of September and October are the most festive months for Telangan. There are two major festivals celebrated during these months and at least 15 days before and after are filled with the aura of great festivity and happy moods of family reunions. One of the festivals is Batukamma and the other is Dusshera (known as Vijaya Dashami and Dusshera etc., this is a popular festival across the nation). However, Batukamma is unique to Telangana region and it is undoubtedly an icon of cultural identity for Telangan. This festival is not celebrated else where, though there are some known instances of festivals celebrated in association with water and flowers, none of them resemble this one. Batukamma comes during the latter half of monsoon, much before the onset of winter. The monsoon rains would have brought plenty of water into the 'cheruvulu' (fresh water ponds that are a major source of irrigation throughout Telangana) and the wild flowers bloom in various vibrant colors all across the uncultivated and barren plains of the region. The most abundant of these are the 'gunuka poolu' and 'tangedi poolu'. There are other flowers too like the banti, chemanti, nandi-vardhanam etc. The 'shilpakka pandlu' (or 'sitpala pandlu') are another great attraction of these barren lands during this season.

The Batukamma grows in size and the bigger it is the better. The white gunuka flowers are colored using water paints and Batukamma gets colorful circular layers of them along with tangedi in between. Then it placed in front of the deity of the home and prayed. As evening approaches the womenfolk dress colorfully with the best of their attire and put on lot of ornaments and place the Batukamma in their 'vaakili' (court yard). The women of neighborhood also join with their own as "Batukammalu" and all of them gather in a large circle around it. They sing songs by going around it building a beautiful human circle of unity, love, sisterhood. They all sing in chorus after a lead singer starts off and the rhythms of the folklore songs reverberate in the neighborhood sounding the uniqueness of Telangana cultural identity. After playing around the "Batukammalu", before the onset of dusk, the women folk carry them on their heads and go as a procession towards a bigger water lake of the village or town. The procession is extremely colorful with the decorations of women and the "Batukammalu". Songs of folklore are sung in chorus throughout the procession and the streets resonate with them. Finally when they reach the water pond the "Batukammalu" are slowly immersed into water after some more playing and singing. Then they share the 'maleeda' (a dessert made with sugar or raw sugar and corn bread) sweets amongst the family members and mneighborhood folks. They return back to their homes with empty 'taambaalam' singing songs in praise of Batukamma. The songs of Batukamma echo in the streets until late night during the entire week.

Bonalu Festival

Bonalu comes from the word "Bonam" which means Bojanaalu or meal in Telugu language. This is an offering to the Goddess Mahankali. The main ritual is offering made by women. Bonalu, also known as Bonalu jatara, is an annual festival celebrated with gusto in Telengana regions of Andhra Pradesh. It is also known as Mahankali jatara or Mahankali Bonalu Jatara, for the main deity of the festival is Goddess Mahankali. Bonalu is one of the important events of Ujjaini Mahankali temple in the twin cities of Secundrabad and Hyderabad. It is celebrated in the month of Ashadha, according to the south Indian calendar. Different places of Telangana celebrates Bonalu on different dates. Generally nevery Sunday of the month of Ashadha masam is celebrated as Bonalu.

They bring cooked rice with sugar, milk and put some onions in an earthen pot. The pot is decorated with small neem branches and a lamp is placed on the top. Turmeric and vermilion is applied to the pot. This whole thing is called Bonam. Women place these pots on their heads and walk to the temple amid the sound of drummers. They are led by dancing men called poturajus. This procession is called jatara. Many other women come to the procession decorating themselves in silk saris and jewelers. Tranced women dance with bonams to the rhythmic beats of drums. This is in the honor of the local goddess Mahankali.

Muharram (Peerla Panduga)

The Muslims pray their respects to the heros who fought against evil. Which commemorates the battle of Karbalath Iraq. In battle the grandson of prophet mohammad was killed and Hindus take part of this festival. Irrespective of caste and cread they performed the peerilu festival.

The processions of peerilu decorated Tazias are taken out in which people of all communities participate. A peeri is prepared with bamboo strips in adome shape. It is covered with glittering clothes. A bamboo pole is fixed in the dome to handle the peeri and at the top metallic cresent of palm shape is attached to it. Finally it is garland with flowers and coconut.

Art and Artists

Thota Vaikuntam

Thota Vaikuntam hails from Andhra Pradesh, in South India, and finds his inspiration in the rural areas of the state. Men and women of his village are often the central characters of his work. Telangana women, in particular, are frequent subjects for his works. The sob session can be traced back to his childhood, when he used to be fascinated by the male artists who used to impersonate female characters in the traveling theatre groups that performed in his village. He admits finding the women of his village very sensuous and that he only attempts to capture their vibrancy.

T. Vaikuntam completed a Diploma in Painting at the College of Fine Arts and Architecture, Hyderabad, in 1970, and then another in Painting and Printmaking from the Faculty of Fine Arts at Maharaja Sayajirao University, Baroda, in 1972. The Hindu revivalist spirit started itself from the time of the sun gas and reached its highest watermark during the gupta and post-gupta periods. With in Hinduism, the two sects, Vaishnavism and Shaivism, were fully developed in their mythology, philosophy and iconography. A new kind of temple architecture, both structural and rock-hewn was evolved which was in tune with the religious needs of the times.

K. Laxma Goud (Printmaker)

Born in 1940 in Nizampur, Andhra Pradesh, K. Laxma Goud completed his diploma in Drawing and Painting from the Government School of Art and Architecture, Hyderabad, in 1963; he then went on to study Mural Painting and Printmaking at the Faculty of Fine Arts at M.S. University, Baroda, from 1963 to 1965. Goud displays versatility over a range of mediums, from printmaking, drawing, water colour, gouache and pastels to glass painting and sculpture in bronze and terracotta.

Goud's work is dramatic; his protagonists are raw and vivacious in their appeal, imbibed with energy that reverberates through his strokes and textures. Most of Goud's art is centered on the rural, recreating landscapes from his childhood as if they were frozen in time. In the artist's later work, his figures turn softer, more introspective than brash in their outlook. Recently, the artist has worked on a series of lush landscapes in vivid colors reminiscent of his youth spent in rural Andhra Pradesh. Like most of the artist's work, these are generally executed in a miniature format.

Yadagiri Rao Breathes Life Into Stone

Yadagiri was born in 1940 in Hyderabad and studied here. "he was new when he was very young that he wanted to be a sculptor. When he was a kid, he was always surrounded stones and carved and chiseled them when my friends were playing,"says Yadagiri Raó. Well, these early carvings lead to greater things. Yadagiri Rao started his artistic journey in the early 1960s. The Telangana Martyrs memorial situated in Gunpark in front of the Assembly is also one of his masterpieces. Yadagiri evolved a newvisual language of sculpture in granite. "Granite is my favorite material. It never gets eroded and never dies out. It stays on forever," Rao says. The time each piece Takes to sculpt depends on the material used and the designs on it. Yadagiri rao another famous works The statue of Durgabai Deshmukh on the Tank Bund, the Ambedkar statue at Karimnagar, the statue of the horse and the flag at Indira park all these and more are the handiwork of Aekka Yadagiri Rao.

Conclusion

On the basis of telangana and iconographic variations, tentative chronological frame work has been suggested. Religious propagation was very effectively carried out through visual arts. In my paper discuss about social function of art has been high lightened, because it is the plastic art through the medium of painting and rock which is the finest expression of culture; the crystallizer of human mind and impulses. It is the barometer which revels the organic growth of culture layer by layer like the palimpsest. Thus the plastic arts play a positive role in the evolution Indian culture and provide an underlying unity to the society throughout the history of India.

REFERENCES

1. Gudimalla Bharath Bhushan: *Bathukamma Magazine*, Namasthe telangaana newspaper, published, 25/09/ 2011, pages all.
2. K. Venkatanagalashmi : telangana lo bathukamm panduga, *Janpada saraswathi,* published, andharapradesh *Janapada Sahitya Parishat hyderabad* 2010, page 147-153.
3. Nayani Krishnakumari: *Bathukamma festival, Janapada Sahitya Parishat,* Potti Sree ramulu Telugu University 1996. Telugu University press published: 1996, 2000.
4. Georg Wilhelm Friedrich *Hegel,* The critical historians of art by Michael Pedro, published in 1982, new haven; Yale university press, New York.
5. *Allam Narayana*: *Bangari Bathukamma,* www.Telangana development forum / literature, Accessed; January 12, 2013.

Movies/Books

1. Kalogi Narayana rao, NAA GODAVA
2. Bathukamma (telugu movie) directed by T. Prabhakar, *Release date*: 2008.
3. Jeevitha Chakram (Telugu movie) Directed by C.S RAO. (1971).

CHAPTER – 11

Festivals in Telangana : A Selected Study

SOMAPANGU MUTHYALAIAH

Introduction

Festivals are an important part of the Telangana culture. The Telangana festivals are in accordance with the happenings and products of nature emerging from different seasons. During the festivals times diverse forms of garment wearing appearance, decoration, preparation of eatables such as area specific dishes and sweets are in vougue. People of Telangana could have migrated to various places across the country and the world, people should follow their traditions during festivals. Some people expand the Telangana festivals culture in various places like continents and Foreign countries. Peoples of Telangana to Participate in Bakrid and Moharam festivals in large numbers as historical tradition. Many temples in Telangana located at bank river of Krishna, Godavari, are decorated with beautiful manner. The most famous festivals in Telangana called : Dussehra, (Bathukamma) Deepavali, Holi, Ramzan, Moharram, Vinayaka Chavithi, Sadar Panduga, Shivarathri, Ugadi, Sriramanavami, Bonala Festival, Rakhi festival etc. Here wrote about some important festivals in Telangana.

Dussehra Festival

Vijayadasami also known as Dasara. The word Vijayadasami is derived from Sanskrit word Vijaya – dasami, which means "Victory on the day of dasami". Ashwayuja Sudha Padyami to Ashwayuja sudha navami 9 days performing Devi navaratrulu. Tenth (10th) day Vijayadasami called Dasara.

This festival is celebrated by all castes people across the Telangana with great devotion. People eagerly searching for Quail bird in the evening as glancing that particular bird Palapitta is considered to be auspicious. The peoples of Telangana collect the leaves of Banni tree also called Jammi Chettu for blessing among themselves. The festival next day lunch is prepared for friends and relatives in the name of Alai Balai. At that time relatives and Friends are enjoing.

Bathukamma Festival

In Telangana before Dasara nine (9) days Amavasya to Navami played a Bathukamma Festival. This festival celebrated by women. This festival is a symbol of Telangana cultural identity. This festival from September to October in every year women decorate Bathukamma with leaves and flowers and worship with devotion. Many varieties of flowers like Thangedu, Lotus, Sunflower, Gummadi, Gunugu, Katla, Nuvvu, Beera, Ganneru etc. are used. Among these, the most important flower called Tangedu using a large. During Bathukamma nine days women clean up their front yard and paste it with cow dug and keep line drawings. At the middle of the location the Bathukamma prepared with flowers and leaves is kept and women encircle it by singing a Bathukamma songs.

Sadar Festival

Mahisha Festival now called as Sadar Festival. This festival is celebrated three days after the deepavali Festival. A buffalo is decorated with anklets, turmeric and bring out in a procession. This festival is celebrated by Yadava Community.

Bonalu Festival

In Telangana the people celebrates Bonalu Festival. Bonalu is one of the Folk Festival, with worshipped mother Goddess Mahankali. Bonalu the word derived from Bonam which means Bojanam (meal). This is an offering to the Goddess Mahankali. Bonalu Festival popularly celebrated in twincities in Telangana. This festival is celebrated during Ashaada Masam (July and August). Women bring cooked rice with sugar, milk and put some onions in an earthern pot. The pot is decorated with small neem branches and a lamp is placed on the top, turmeric and vermilion is applied to the pot. This total event is called Bonam. The Bonalu Festival starts on the first Sunday of Ashadam begin at Golconda Fort, then followed by Ujjain Mahankali temple in Secunderabad and Balkampet Yellamma temple on Second Sunday. Potharaju the brother of mother goddess is represented in recessions by a well built bare-bodied man wearing a small tightly draped red dhoti and bells on his ankles and anointed within turmeric on his body and vermillion on his forehead. Potharaju dances to the resounding drums and dances close to Palaharam bandi. Rangam is performing the oracle is held after the next morning of the actual festival. In 1815, a devotee by name Narsaiah went to Ujjain as a soldier and witnessed many diseases aroung him at the new place. These diseases could not effect him and he believed it as a blessing of Goddess. Narsaiah brought along with an idol of Mahankali from Ujjain. The devotee established the idol in an architectural temple at Secunderabad and performed Bonalu every year.

Peerla Festival

The Muslims pray their respects to the heros who fought against evil. Which commemorates the battle of Karbalath Iraq. In battle the grandson of prophet mohammad was killed and Hindus take part of this festival. Irrespective of caste and cread they performed the peerilu festival.

The processions of peerilu decorated Tazias are taken out in which people of all communities participate. A peeri is prepared with bamboo strips in adome shape. It is covered with glittering clothes. A bamboo pole is fixed in the dome to handle the peeri and at the top metallic cresent of palm shape is attached to it. Finally it is garland with flowers and coconut.

Holi Festival

This festival is celebrated with culture of North – Indian. During this festival people spray colours on each other irrespective of age and community. In the afternoon and evening people make a drink with certain natural products called "Bhangu" and consume it.

Polala Amavasya Festival

Thi festival is celebrated in the beginning of Bhadrapada masam, particularly in August and September, people observe this day on a new moon day. Polala amavasya is dedicated to Goddess Poleramma. All the Families of agriculture communities collect red soil and paste it on bulls and cows and clean them to worship. During this festival time several mantras or prayers dedicated to Goddess Shakti like 'Durga Stuti'. This festival is celebrated in all the villages in Telangana.

Deepavali

This Festival is celebrated during month of October. This is most popular Hindu Festival. Diwali symbolizes the spiritual victory of light over darkness good over evil and knowledge. This festival is widely associated with Lakshmi, goddess of prosperity. Some of the business classes celebrated Kubera puja and Lakshmi Narayana Puja.

Christmas

Every year on December 25th is celebrated Christmas festival worshipped Lord Jesus Christ. All Christian people decoreated their houses with coloring during the time Christmas and January first festivals and performed the prayer to Jesus Christ. This occasion people cut cakes and distribute among themselves and wish happiness and prosperity to all in the eve of new year.

Sammakka – Sarakka Jatara

This Jatara celebration by the tribal people of Tadvai mandal, Medaram (vil), in Prof. Jayashankar Bhopalpally District. Medaraju was a contemporary of the Kakatiya king Rudradeva. He ruled polavasa kingdom. His daughter sammakka marriage with Pagidigiddaraju. He ruled medaram region. He had three children called Saralamma, Nagulamma, Jampanna. Pagidigiddaraju not paid the tax to Kakatiya rulers because severe famines for four years. Prataparudra – I declared the war on Medaram region. Pagidigiddaraju entire family bravely fight against the Kakatiya's army. All of them got killed in the battle. Jampanna also fought bravely till his last breath and died in "Sampanga Vagu. Sampangavagu now called Jampanna Vaagu. The people celebrate the Medarama Jatara. The Medaram Jatara is organized once in two years. It is three day fair. The people offer Bangaram Jaggery to the goddesses.

Conclusion

The state of Telangana has many districts Folk-lore art forms. All the festivals mark collective living, and community culture.

The festivals Spirituality entertainment, Fun and friendship during the festivals. Telangana has culturally a unique and diversified culture. The people of Telangana proudly claim that these festivals are related to their culture. Finally the Telangana Festivals celebrated in accordance with the happiness and products of nature emerging from different seasons.

There are many another festsivals like lumbini festival Budha Jayanthi. Kakatiya festival in Warangal, Kite festival, Satavahana festival etc. are celebrated in different months. These total festivals motivate people to spread love and affection and to strength among the peoples. Festivals promote good human relations among the people.

REFERENCESS

1. Barry Pavier, The Telangana Movement 1944-1951, Vikas Publishing house Pvt. Ltd 1981, New Delhi.
2. Simhadri S and Jayashankar K., Talladillutunna Telangana, Hyderabad, Centre for Telangana Studies, 2000.
3. G. Venkata Ramarao, Telangana Charitra.
4. Ramesan, Freedom Struggle in Hyderabad.
5. I. Thirumali, Telangana – Andhra, 2013.
6. P. Sundaraiah, Telangana peoples struggle and its lessons, Calcutta, 1992.
7. D.N. Dhanagare, Peasant movement in India 1920-50.
8. Raza Alikhan, Hyderabad 400 years.
9. Thadakamalla Vivek and others, 1969 Movement-Historical documents, Telangana history – society, Hyderabad, 2009.
10. Adiraju Venkateswar Rao – Telangana Rashtrodhyamaalu, 2014.

CHAPTER – 12

Mutiny of 1857 in Hyderabad: Causes and Results

JALLA ARUNA

Introduction

The First War of Independence in 1857 (or the Sepoy Mutiny as the British preferred to describe it) was mostly confined to Meerut, Delhi, Lucknow, Kanpur, Barrackpore, Gwalior, Jhansi, Arrah and few other areas. However, some isolated incidents took place at other areas in the country too. These were quickly suppressed. Hyderabad too was witness to one of its own. We cannot forget the role of Turrebaz Khan, who attacked the castle of the British Residency in Hyderabad. The uprising of 1857 in Hyderabad, led by Turrebaz Khan and Maulvi Allauddin, was essentially to free Jamedar Cheeda Khan, who was held as a prisoner inside the Residency. Though high-school history books have omitted the story, there was a significant impact of the revolt of 1857 on Hyderabad too. As the news of the revolt, which started in Meerut reached Hyderabad, posters appeared on walls of mosques, churches and in public squares, urging the Nizam and the people to rise up against the British. "But unfortunately Nizam Afzal Ud-daula and his minister, Salar Jung along with the Umraos and Sardars, adopted a pro-British stance.

1857 Revolt of Hyderabad – Causes

Afjal-ud-Daula of Asaf-Zahi clan became the 5th king in 1857. He inherited Salar Jung who was an exceptionally able administrator as his Minister. The fifth Nizam ruled Hyderabad only for 12 years. No other Nizam ruled for such a short period. Even then, in this brief spell, some very important events took place. India faced a powerful explosive situation during the very first year of his ascension. British people took more than hundred years to secure their place in India. Under their authoritarian dispensation the conservative Indians were highly dissatisfied and it resembled fire covered by water. During this period the peasants lost their lands and they became laborers. Craftsmen had to leave their customary professional work. Employees became unemployed. The revenue administration of the British left a deep dissatisfaction among the people of Indian village system. Corruption in Revenue and Police Departments caused people to suffer. When the English brought more or less the whole of India under their rule they remained at a distance from the local rulers and kings. The kings of the Samasthanams (States/Estates) were crushed under their administrative system. The succession system introduced by Dalhousie mainly evoked deep distrust of the local rulers. Their sneaky tricks and tactics to encroach upon the Samasthanaas adopted by them bought rivalry against them. The highly acclaimed Moghul sovereign Bahadursha Zaffar was forcibly removed from Red Fort and was ordered by Dalhousie to spend his time in Mehrauli. Lord Canning proclaimed Bahadursha Zafar to be the last Emperor and that his successors will not be able to inherit his titles. The haughtiness of the British was a severe blow to the self-respect of the great Mughals who ruled India for nearly 300 years. The rulers of the Samasthanaas became suspect of the intentions of the British rulers and were afraid of their own future. The Hindus were worried about religious conversions by the Christian Missionaries in the name of Education. More than all others, the Indian Soldiers (Sepoys) faced torture and ignominy. Difference in matters of promotions, pay and allowances, between a British soldier and their Indian counterparts led to test their patience. On the whole, the dissatisfaction in all respects in various ways among the Indians reached a flash point and they were ready to start a fire. A spark of fire was enough to set a forest in fire. Enfield rifle provided that. Mutiny first started in Meerut. There was not enough time for them to work out a system to contain the intensity. Many fled away due to this. Recovering from this soon they started battles to defend themselves. At this point of time assistance from the rulers of Samasthanams was available to them.

Unlike in North India, the revolt did not start in Hyderabad instantly. Though begun late, it vented their extreme displeasure towards the British here also. In the South the English Government was most sensitive and was in a state of equilibrium. There was no dearth of antagonism in Hyderabad against the British. Firstly, Alija and his friends Sadasiva Reddy and Raja Mahipatiram tried armed rebellion in different times. The offshoot of these inimical ideas was the origin of Mubaarij-Ud-Daula and his close associates. The Wahabi movement initiated by Abdul WahabNejdi of Saudi to resurrect the greatness of Islam entered India in 1820 with Peshawar in Afghanistan as the center of the movement. Here this became an opposing force against the English Rule and the propaganda of the Christian kaffirs. The person who started this movement in India was Sayyad Ahmed Brailvi. In Hyderabad this movement was carried on by Mujari-Ud-Daula son of Nasiruddoula and his followers and by Ghulam Rasool Khan

Nawab of Kurnool against the British. Mujari-Ud-Daula was caught and was imprisoned. His followers were also imprisoned but were released much earlier than 1857. They were successful in spreading hatred against the British. Biraar which was a part of the Nizam kingdom was occupied by the English in 1853. As a result, the financial condition of the Nizam nosedived. Nizam became helpless being unable to repay the debts to the English. British needed cotton grown in Birar and hence annexed it to feed the Textile mills in England. People could not bear this indignity. Loss of Kurnool and Birar made them to suffer ignominy. They did not forget the death of Tippu Sultan in Mysore. In Kerala Mopla Muslims were revolting inspired by the Wahabis. Muslims of Madras were also thinking of following suit. At this time the followers of Tantiya Tope were roaming in Hyderabad wearing the robes of mendicants and saints and preaching against the British. Many soldiers lost jobs as the Government army was disbanded. Many soldiers nurtured hatred against British as they lost jobs due to the British. Some of the Amirs also exhibited enmity against the British.

As the revolt was spreading like wildfire in North India, the British wished and tried to salvage at least South India from the flames. Among nearly 500 Samasthanams in the country, Hyderabad was the largest Samasthanam. This was like the heart of South India. If there is revolt in the Nizam's kingdom it can convert the area from Nagpur to Madras as an auto clave. If the Nizam of Hyderabad Samasthanam with 15 per cent Muslim population supported their cause, the entire Muslim population of South India would be ready to revolt. There are Tamils, Kannadigas and Marathis in large numbers in the Hyderabad State. If they also participated in the revolt, there was every chance that people of Marathwada, Madras, and Mysore also joined the bandwagon. In this delicate situation the British feared that unless the Nizam of Hyderabad came to their help, he might join hands with the mutineers, and the unhappy cadres could not be crushed. At one stage, the Resident was worried that if 'Nizam was lost, then everything was lost'. In this complex situation they decided to save at least the Hyderabad Samasthanam (State). They closely observed the decisions taken by the Nizam and tried to contain him. They schemed in such a way that the Nizam was entrapped. They told him that they would write off the loan given to the Nizam and return Birar to the Nizam once the revolt was brought to an end. True to their scheming, the Nizam decided to be generous to them and proclaimed his trustworthiness. Not alone that, at the time of his death Naasir-ud-daula advised his son to be loyal to the English. As a result, due to the maneuvering and planning of his minister, he kept Hyderabad safe for the British from the Mutineers.

By 1857 the Hyderabad Army was reduced to a large extent. The battalion consisted only of about 30,000 men. It was in a state of disorder and for lack of training it was weak. Most of the soldiers were hired ones. The Hyderabad Contingent had 10,000 soldiers. There were about 80 European officers to command them. This was an organized army, duly trained and was armed with weapons. Nevertheless it was not that it had no traitors. Now and then such events were being repeated. The agents of Wahabi movement who instigated religious ideas and secured the loyalty of soldiers are an example of this. The reason for this was the vicious behavior, levity against the soldiers, disrespectful behavior and the non-discriminate admonitions by the European officers was hurting them too much. Captain Abbat belonging to the First Cavalry Regiment was not allowing Muslim soldiers to do prayers of offering

Namaz. Muharram processions, and 'Matham', public grief was forbidden by Brigadier Meckangie. These were unbearable to the Muslim soldiers. It led to the emotional outrage and hatred of the soldiers. Mullahs and Maulvies took advantage of this situation and stoked fire. Along with that the Amirs and Landlords, out of anger against Nizam and the British encouraged the revolutionaries.

Among the population of the town, Sikhs, Sindhias, Africans, persons of Turkish origin, Iranians, Turanians and the hybridized progeny of the Mughals were living. They used to be armed with weapons and were brave. Salaar Jung deployed strong Arab army to suppress the incidence of isolated convective churning.

Within a month of ascension to the throne by Afzal-Ud-Daula, many posters appeared on the walls of the capital. The poster on the wall contained the words – 'if you decide to kill a kaffir but delay the action, you will be excommunicated from the Muslim society'. Some of the posters said that it was better for Tahaniyat Ali Khan Bahadur Afjal-Ud-Daula to gather all the Muslims and suppress the Kaffirs and then to go to Delhi and that he would get help from Allah and support by the Prophet in this. The poster also said that unless the king and the minister (Diwan) joined the movement, they would end up being road repair workers within a year. These said that there is a diktat by the Prophet that Afzal-Ud-Daula must read this notice and that the public should read the same and unless they do that their progeny of seven generations would become cursed. These notices stating the above were appearing on the walls of all Masjids and in all populous areas. Encouraging people to announce Jihad against the British started. To bring stability in Deccan, to announce Jihad against British, one must trust Islam's Mohammed Mustafa Sullula, Allah Vosulul' after reading this notice. Maulvies must issue Fatwas asking Jamindars and Khajis to announce war against the English men and if they do not do that, their heirs would become a cursed lot. It was also said that the persons hearing this have to inform the matter to the King and the Diwan. Poor, Rich, Maulvi, Kaji, Mufti, Kotwal, and Subedar, anyone of these opposing kaffirs would become a Ghaji (a knight). If he dies in the cause he would find a place in sacred worlds. It was decided that all Muslims would congregate in Mecca Masjid on Friday the 25thShaval 1273, and move on from there. If anybody fails to come to this Jihad their next seven generations would be excommunicated. Rage against the English united the Hindus and Muslims at this time. Upon seeing this turn of events, fear gripped among the English. They tried to mobilize army. Hyderabad was then having two types of military one was contingent and another Nizam's army.

The Contingent Army was stationed at Elichpur, Aurangabad, Mominabad, Gulbarga, Hingoli, Bollaram, Warangal, Makhtal, Lingusugur, and Buldana's hilly tracts for protection. This used to move from these places to the places where they were required. The Nizam's Army of Native soldiers consisted of not more than 30,000 men. These were under Jamedars. The Jamedars were mostly Sikhs, Arabs, and Rohillas. This Army was not being used mostly.

Col. Davidson became the Resident in 1857 due to the death of Rushibi. The unrest was peaking and was ready to erupt at this time in Hyderabad. Leaders surfaced. One among them was Maulvi Ibrahim. He was lecturing in Masjids and inciting people. He admonished the Maulvi who was speaking as to why he was behaving like a woman? If you have no courage you may wear bangles and sit down. If you have the courage you will talk about the Jihad against foreign oppression. He shouted 'Tell that both Nizam and Diwan should put down the English

Government'. Instantly there were counter shouts 'din' 'din'. Immediately the Kotwal tried to suppress them. He escaped. Rioters were creating disturbances in Masjids during nights. Salaar Jung deployed Arab Forces to suppress them. They used to frisk and thoroughly check any person coming to or going out of the city. They were ensuring that no more than 20 persons assembled at one point. Another leader was Khamosh Shah. He was a Fakir belonging to a higher class. His followers joined hands with Maulvi Abdullah and Maulvi Allah-ud-din and spread ideas of treason among people and the associate army known as 'BoyinapalliFouz'. A frightened Col. Davidson asked the Diwan to punish them. As a result, Maulvi Ibrahim was arrested and produced before the Nizam. Having been admonished seriously by the Nizam he escaped incognito. Nevertheless the decision of Nizam and the speed at which the Minister worked were of no avail. Chinks appeared in the loyalty of BoyinapalliFouz. They moved about without permission of their officers and without passports in Hyderabad streets and preached that time had come to agitate against all the Europeans.

Misbehavior of personal security guards of the Resident belonging to the Seventh Madras Cavalry added further fuel to the defeat of the British. Even while performing ordained duty they indulged in treasonable conversations. The Resident observed 'In the view of National Government, it was shameful and deplorable that even the representative of the Governor General in the Nizam's Court was unable to believe his own personal security guards. Resident was unable to believe his own associate army. On the whole except for the Third Cavalry, the capital city neared the exploding situation. But then the explosion took place sooner.

The mutiny of 1857 in Hyderabad can be gauged from three angles –

1. Rebellion by the Aurangabad Contingent Force,
2. Attack on the Residency, and
3. The rebellion and conspiracy in different places of the State.

Rebellion by the Aurangabad Contingent Force

Due to the critical condition in North Central India, British deployed as many men as they could mobilize from the month of May. There could not be an exception for deploying the Subsidiary Contingent Army of Hyderabad. They had to send the Third Cavalry belonging to Hyderabad to Malegaon on the request of the Bombay Government. In their place the contingent of First Cavalry under Capt. H.D. Abbatt was sent on 11th June 1857 from Mominabad to Aurangabad. When the First Cavalry reached Chota Pimpalgaon which was 14 kilometers away from Aurangabad, the Horse-riders and other army men determined that as a part of a conspiracy they were being sent to a faraway Aurangabad. They reached Aurangabad and were lodged among the cavalries in Kala Chabutra. There another incident happened to augment their doubt. Capt. Abbatt decided to verify the horses and accordingly sent word to Regiment Risaladar Mohammed Buran. It was clear to the cavalrymen that Aurangabad was not their destination but that they would be required to travel longer distances. With that they became furious. They started chanting the name of Mughal Emperor. They shouted the slogan that 'We won't go out of Nizam's boundary – *'Deenkeuparkamarnahibandenge'*.Thus on 14th June Abbatt called a meeting of all Jamedars and ordered the Cavalry to be shifted to Amba. The Cavalry and the Infantry were separated and they were lodged separately near the river Kaum in Amba. For security reasons the officers sent their families away to safer places. He sent messages to Poona and

Maggur for help. There were secret parleys, signals and meetings between the Infantry and the Cavalry. On 14th June Burhanbooks of the Third Cavalry informed Abbatt that the soldiers waved green flag. By then additional forces under the command of Woodburn came from Ahmednagar by 24th June 1857. In that powerful, strong and valiant men, 14 light dragoons, cannons behind European gunmen and 25 Bombay Infantry were brought. Mutineers were lined up and their names read out in the first troop. First was Jamedar Amir Khan. When his name was read out, there was commotion among the soldiers. Woodburn fired on them. Immediately inquiry was conducted. Many of the cavalrymen of the First and Second Cavalry were declared guilty. They were disarmed. Amir Khan among them escaped. DafedarFida Ali fired at Abbatt but missed the target. Fida Ali was hanged after a trial proceeding. One Risaladar, three Jamedars, nine Dafedars, 76 Troopers and four Trumpet blowers were involved in the whole incident. Out of these 21 persons were fired upon and killed. Three persons were fired with guns. Some of them were exiled. Some were whipped. Some were removed from service. Betrayal Regiment Divisions were deprived of weapons, released and sent.

Cavalrymen belonging to the Third Cavalry who went to Buldana became angry after coming to know the developments. The Third Cavalry of Hyderabad went to Buldana under the command of Lt. Lenox. There he was met by Capt. Gall, belonging to 25 Bombay Native Infantry, with his forces. This caused outrage in the Third Cavalry. 13 persons out of them escaped from Buldana under the leadership of Jamedar Chidakhan and ran away to reach Hyderabad after 20 days in July. They hoped that Hyderabad Government will save them. But then the Hyderabad Government announced a reward of 3000 on Chidakhan. When they entered Hyderabad, Salar Jung arrested them and sent to Residency for further trial. They arrested the followers of Chidakhan.

Attack on the Residency

The news of arrest of Chidakhan and his followers spread like wildfire in the city. People congregated in Masjids and made emotional speeches. Salar Jung sent the Arab troops and dispersed the groups, but informed the Resident that Residency might be attacked. Those who arranged the congregations decided to send four Maulvies to the King and pray to release Chidakhan and his associates and that if the king did not agree, to attack the Residency. When their desire was not fulfilled they were ready to attack the Residency on the 17th July 1857. Salar Jung came to know beforehand that the Residency might be attacked. He initiated steps to meet the situation. Contingent troops lodged in different bases of Hyderabad were retained to the extent of requirement of different branches and removed the rest. Six cannons and one Cavalry squad were shifted to the Residency. He mobilized additional men and armory of three cannons, two mortars, one Detailed Cannon firemen, one cavalry troop, and 25 troopers belonging to Madras Light Infantry and 200 foot soldiers of Madras Regiment. Each and every entry point of the Residency was fitted with bayonets.

Different officers were posted in different directions.

- Lt. Col. S.C. Briggs – Military Secretary to have overall control.
- Capt. George Holms – Control of Madras Horse Artillery.
- Capt. Allen Scott – To command the Hyderabad Contingent guns
- Capt. Bradley, 24th Regiment – To protect Madras troops

- Major Thornhill and Capt. Campbell – Volunteers for the first and second assistants of the Resident.

In this way Col. Davidson turned the Residency into a Fort. Salar Jung informed Col. Davidson that the people assembled in Mecca Masjid proclaimed Jihad and rioting may start around 1 0' clock on 17th July Friday. But this did not happen. At about 6 p.m. Salar Jung sent a spy to inform that 500 Rohillas under the leadership of Turrebaaz khan and Allauddin were coming towards the Residency. Salar Jung thought that Davidson would get ready and that in the meanwhile Nizam army could be deployed.

At 6 p.m. 600 armed men marched towards the Residency. Jamedar Turrebaaz khan led this group. Roads leading toThe Residency virtually turned into a sea of militant mutineers. Each and every gate of the Residency was closed. All entry points were arranged with patrol teams with guns. Resident adopted self-protection strategy.

Rohillas annexed two structures on the western side of the Residency, one belonging to Jaigopal Das and the second to Abbin Sahib. Both of them were traders. They also occupied the area towards Dilsukh Gardens. From the occupied places they urged the Indian guards at the Residency Gate to secure release of Jamedar Chidakan and his associates. The mutineers thought that the Indian guards will join the mutineers. But then, Risaldar Ismail Khan came forward to talk about the misadventure of the militants. They were surprised that Ismail Khan should show loyalty to the foreign masters. They fired at him. He escaped. Residency Commander S.C. Briggs's strategy was not to attack the militants that night. The Arab Guards regiment sent by Salar Jung surrounded the buildings under the control of the mutineers. Rohillas broke open the walls adjoining the occupied buildings and started a ferocious attack on the

Residency. In this attack the Putlibowlie gate collapsed. Firing went on for about half an hour. Briggs retaliated with cannon fire. He continued the fire till 4 a.m. in the early morning. When the retaliation was such severe, the Rohillas escaped into darkness having nothing else to do. They were helped by the Arab Guards. 32 men of Madras Artillery died of gunfire and injuries. Militant leaders Turrebaazkhan and Maulvi Allauddin were declared offenders. On them 5000 was announced as reward. While Turrebaazkhan was on the run on 22nd July he was arrested at Mogulaguda and was produced in the Karmat Ali Magistrate Criminal Court. Civil Court Magistrate Fazlulla recorded their statements. While he was being shifted to Andaman having been punished with life imprisonment he escaped at Mogiligidda in Mehboobnagar district. He was again arrested near Toopran with the help of Kurbaan Ali. He died while resisting the arrest. His body was brought to Kothi in Hyderabad and he was hanged. Maulvi Allauddin fled away to Bangalore. There he was caught at Mangalapalli and was tried. He was awarded punishment of life imprisonment and sent to Andaman on 28th June 1859. He died there in 1884. Thus the attack on the Residency by the Mutineers failed for lack of cooperation from the countrymen.

The Rebellion and conspiracy in different places of the State

The rebellion did not end with the attack on the Residency. Somewhere or other the rebels were creating disturbances in different parts of the State till the year 1860. Critical condition arose with Nana Sahib, Tantiya Tope and Rao sahib Peeshwa going to people and preaching. People's anger against the British was given further Philip by this preaching and this was vented through rebellion and conspiracy in some parts of the State.

Among these the first to show up was that of Raja Venkatappa Naik of Shorapur in the matter of paying tax to the Nizam.

Reasons for the failure of the Rebellion

The mutiny failed because of lack of competent leadership, unity, and organizational strength. Added to this, the Nizam and Salar Jung sided with the British. British did not ignore this. As a measure of gratitude, firstly Raichur, Antarvedi, Naldurg districts were handed over to the Nizam. These districts taken over in 1853 from the Nizam to maintain the Hyderabad Contingent were returned. They retained only Birar under their control. The Shorapur Estate was given to the Nizam. They also forfeited the debt of 50 lakhs. They entered into a new agreement in 1860 suitably modifying the first agreement. Not only that, the Nizam was gifted ten thousand pound sterling and Salar Jung was given presents worth the value of three thousand sterling. The Nizam also, true to his standing and reputation, sent gifts to the Governor General valuing fifteen thousand pound sterling. They announced the title 'The Star of India' to the Nizam. But people opposed this and expressed their protest through posters and handbills throughout the city against the Nizam and the Diwan.

Result of the mutiny

With the crushing of the mutiny, the Mughal Empire which was in existence for namesake only ended. The last Mughal Emperor was sent to Burma. The Governor General advised the Nizam to come up with his own currency and coins. Nizam Bahadurshah refused to mint or print currency during his lifetime but the Governor General did not yield. As a result, coins were released with the words 'Nizam-Ul-Mulk Asafza Bahadur' on one side and 'Julus My manath Jarb

Farkundabuniyad Hyderabad' on the other side. These were called 'haalisikka' Khutban was being read not in the name of the Emperor but in the name of Afjaluddoula. Not only that, the post of Mughal Subedar in the Hyderabad Nizam's Court was abolished. In fact the Nizam was pressurized into declaring Hyderabad as a sovereign state only to announce that the Mughal Empire ended. But then the loyalty of the British to Hyderabad was suspect. As far as the Nizam was concerned, they behaved as if they were the masters. The First Nizam never even dreamt of declaring Hyderabad a sovereign state. Pressure was brought on the Fifth Nizam and declaration to the effect that it became independent was made. There was meaning to the word independence in 1724. By 1858 that word became meaningless. Though Nizam was independent, he was really not a free bird. The British realized that they would have to make suitable attitude change towards the Samasthanams (States/Estates). The rights, special powers and dignity and respect of the Indian rulers would be treated as the honor and dignity of the British themselves, it was announced. Lands belonging to the mutineers forcibly taken away from them, the titles and other lands were granted to them as a measure of recognition of the loyalty and trustworthiness of the rulers of the States/Estates during 1857 and duly recognizing their valuable services to the British. Imposts were written off. Honors, gifts and presents, and titles were awarded to them. As a part of that the Nizam was being addressed as a trustworthy friend 'Faithful Ally' and 'Yaare Vaffadar' while giving the award of the title 'Grand Commander Star of India'. With that the knighthood of 'Most Exalted Order' was presented.

Even when the Government in England took control of the Company (East India Company) due to the mutiny, there was no change in the relationship between Nizam and the

British. Interference of the British increased even more. Functioning of the sovereign State of Nizam was restricted. In the least the sovereign ruler was not having right and power to appoint or remove his own ministers.

REFERENCES

1. Uprising of 1857: A Movement that defined India of august 15, 1947 (Tura Baz Khan, the Hero of Hyderabad), (2012) Devireddy Subramanyam Reddy.
2. An Era of Darkness: The British Empire in India Hardcover – 27 Oct 2016 Shashi Tharoor.
3. India's Struggle for Independence: 1857-1947 (2016), Bipan Chandra.
4. 30 Indian Freedom Fighters Who Disappeared In the Pages of History, Akarsh Mehrotra.
5. 1857 Uprising: A Tale of an Indian Warrior– (2008) Kaushik Roy.
6. 1857, the Uprising, (2008) Gautam Gupta.
7. The Freedom Struggle in Hyderabad: A Connected Account,
8. The Sepoy Mutiny and the revolt of 1857 (1963), R.C. Majundar.
9. The Great Uprising: India, 1857 (2007), Pramod K Nayar.
10. The Great Fear of 1857: Rumours, Conspiracies and the Making of the Indian Uprising (2014) Kim A. Wagner.
11. 1857 Revisited (2008), S.M.A Hussain.
12. The 1857 Rebellion (2010), Biswamoy Pati.

CHAPTER 13

Telangana Jatharalu : A Historical Study on Peddagattu and Komuravelli Jathara

NAGAMMA SUREPALLY

Introduction

A large number of rural people participate and particular seasonally celebrating the biggest festival is called Jathara.During the fair all the people involved in one place worship deity is worshiped. Based on time, jatharas can be devided into two types celebrating the festivals.

Bonalu Festival

This is special festival in Telangana region. Both men and women are involved in this horoscope.men dance before the bonam with the dress of tiger and pothuraju. Women put new pots

and cook the bonam, decorate this with the yellow saffron and put a lamp on the bonam,hold the neem leaves in hands then bonam is offered to the goddess.

Bathukamma Festival

Bathukamma is a colourful and vibrant festival of Telangana. And celebrated by women with flowers of different colours that glow exclusively in each region. This festival is a symbol of telangana's cultural identity. The most abundant of these are the"gunugu poolu,and thagedi poolu". There are other flowers too like the banthi,chamanthi,nandi vardhaman etc. Decorate Gowridevi with different colors of flowers,in the form of bathukamma. This is the 9days festival and every day has different name.

Moharam (Peerla Panduga)

The Muslims pray their respects to the heros who fought against evil. Which commemorates the battle of Karbalath Iraq. In battle the grandson of prophet mohammad was killed and Hindus take part of this festival. Irrespective of caste and cread they performed the peerilu festival.

The processions of peerilu decorated Tazias are taken out in which people of all communities participate. A peeri is prepared with bamboo strips in adome shape. It is covered with glittering clothes. A bamboo pole is fixed in the dome to handle the peeri and at the top metallic cresent of palm shape is attached to it. Finally it is garland with flowers and coconut.

Sammakka Sarakka Jathara

This Jatara celebration by the tribal people of Tadvai mandal, Medaram (vil), in Prof. Jayashankar Bhopalpally District. Medaraju was a contemporary of the Kakatiya king Rudradeva. He ruled polavasa kingdom. His daughter sammakka marriage with Pagidigiddaraju. He ruled medaram region. He had three children called Saralamma, Nagulamma, Jampanna. Pagidigiddaraju not paid the tax to Kakatiya rulers because severe famines for four years. Prataparudra – I declared the war on Medaram region. Pagidigiddaraju entire family bravely fight against the Kakatiya's army. All of them got killed in the battle. Jampanna also fought bravely till his last breath and died in "Sampanga Vagu. Sampangavagu now called Jampanna Vaagu. The people celebrate the Medarama Jatara. The Medaram

Jatara is organized once in two years. It is three day fair. The people offer Bangaram Jaggery to the goddesses.

Folk Jatharas

People in the rural area, from fime immemorial artifacts they do, like painting, folk dances, folk songs, musical instruments,and the performances they make based on instruments are called folklore these folk reflect the culture traditions the way of life of people living in rural area these does not contain any written evidence.It is hereditary from one generation to another and in the absence of living from time imminent life.some castes believe in these folktales and choose them as a profession and make up some special groups and make art appearances. For example: Budiga jangaalu (baagotham), chindu (Yakshaganam), Pagati veshaalu,sadhana shoorulu etc. Those who live in the life of folklore are the ones who are living in the daytime.All castes in the telangana region usually perform folk arts as part of their way of life. folk arts also perform various festivals, weddings, ceremonies and bad works also. As a part of this, in the gattu jathara and Komuravelli jathara,folk people worship their worship deities according to their customs. Jathara is the folk art generally venue. The folk art show is also a folk art show that is,instruments and sounds especially daps, locks, horns, groans etc. Most of the instruments with rhythmic words are and carefully until the beginning of the horoscope. A map of folklore stopping a folk painting will sit down the favorite God and will be married. The Shiva forces rocks have been mesmerized by themselves and the future says that divine is conducted. Pothurajula dances, tigers, bonuse,ornaments and yellow saffron decorating the lamps, animal sacrifices are all but folk art.some occur once in a year at least a year and once, in two three years. There are also folk worship priest in this folk jathara devotees all over the country come to the folk festivals and submit their offerings and requests.

Komuravelli Jathara

The speciality of this jathara is Renuka yallamma is also deity along with Mallikarjuna Swamy. This is one of important jatharas celebrated in the telangana region. Started in the moth of January during makara Sankranthi -Ugadi,in the day of Sunday and Wednesday of 3 months.

Komuravelli Mallikarjuna Swamy temple popularly known as" Komuravelli Mallanna temple"is located on a hill in Komuravelli village of siddipet district in the state of Telangana. The primary deity is Mallanna or Mallikarjuna Swamy who is an incarnation of lord Shiva. The festive season called as jathara, begins from Sankranthi and lasts till ugadi. Large number of devotees offer prayers to the deity all Sundays which falls between Sankranthi and ugadi. All devotees are sing like Podam Padara Komuravelli jathara and folk are from all parts of the state telangana, from Maharashtra,and karnataka to pray God and is called "Dhooli Dharshanam". As per Mythology Swamy varu enshrined on Indra keeladri in 11th century. One day lord came in a dream of a shepherd and informed him that he made the hill indra keeladri and enshrined in it with "Putta Matti" to

fulfill the desires of the devotees. As per local Mythology that Sri Mallikarjuna married daughter of an yadava community have Golla kethamma and another woman from Linga Balija family by name Medalamma. These two ladies adorned Swamy varu on his both sides in the sanctum and sanetorium.

Peddapatnam

A large portrait of rangoli is called Pedda Patnam. It is put in a wide area and the oggu priests read and chant mantras in common partance to get married to Komuravelli Mallanna and deities. Oggu poojaries from yadava community are attending to perform rituals of "Patnams and Bonams". There is an unique procedure that devotees used to get Patnam (Rangavallies) by oggu priests.

Agni Gundaalu

Large number of devotees visit the Mallanna temple during the Agnigundaalu. Which is celebrated on the Sunday falling before the ugadi. The speciality of skipping fire is here they believe that those who pass the fire, sins will be gone.

Gangiregi Tree

Another important event in this temple, Pradakshina to Gangiregi tree: and offering prayer to vallu banda etc . Are also important and the devotees have belief that their desires such as blessing with wealth etc. After fullfiling of their desire,they used to offer bull which is called Kode kattula. The devotees visiting sri yellamma ammavaru and offer their prayers and they take new pots with yellow saffrons to express their devotional attention. The woman dances with bonam, without any basiss and support. This is the speciality of the jathara. Similarly, this is a narrow paggage between two large boulders called Needle Hamlet in Komuravelli. If they go out of this rug, they feel like

they are safe from all sins and sufferings. And bathing with wet clothes and praising with kneeling before God to give them children who have no children. And this Bathing is called as "Thadibattalu". This whole jathara was conducted by the all, Erra Gollalu,Kuruma Gollalu, and Poojarulu.

Pedda Gattu Jathara

Peddagattu Jathara is one of the second largest jathara in telangana state. Devotees comes from both telugu states and neighboring states of Chattisgarh and Odisha. This is the most celebrated jathara once in two years. And lakhs of devotees are coming to this jathara. Peddagattu Jathara is the festival done in the name of lord lingamanthulu Swamy, and goddess choudamma every 2years. This is the second biggest religious jathara in the state of Telangana after Sammakka Sarakka Jathara Medaram. Primarily the yadava community takes part in huge members people from castes and religions from across Telangana, Andhra Pradesh,Mahartra,Odissa,Karnataka and Tamilnadu. The horoscope has a history of about 1200 years, Dhruvadu a king of state calm, and built the village in his own name that was "Durajpally". This the nearest village of

"Urlugonda" had 7 hills,one of the large hill is called "Peddagattu". In the peddagattu jathara "Lingamanthulu Swamy" is the God of in this temple and worshiped by the most of the yadava devotees,so this jathara is called as "Gollagattu jathara"also. And all the devotees are arrived with the bullock carts, autos,and tractors a day before the event.

Men dressing in this Jathara

Males are wearing red banion and Palms of the legings and palms of their hands. And also "Gajjela Nikker". While they are beating the "Dooluck" it is a folk musical instrument and it gives a sound like "Dillam- Kallem" is in the middle of the rhythm.

Women Devotees

Women are having yellow saffron with wet clothes and decorated with flowers . Who doesn't have the children,bring the "Bonamand sacrifical lamb to the God". Before they arrived the sheep bathed and add the flower stalk,yellow saffron, leaves the nodders sacred.Choudamma she is the sister of Lingamanthulu Swamy,Ganga Bhavani, Yalamanchamma, and Manikyala Devi.

Lingamanthulu Swamy is Vegetarian he is offered only vegenism so the devotees bring and put the bonam at Lingamanthulu Swamy temple. And coming with the loud words of "O linga.. O linga.." Animal sacrifice at Choudamma and Ganga Bhavani,Yallamma deities etc. Peddagattu Jathara celebrated as 5 days jathara. It will start with when the devotees carrying the "Devarapette" (a religious box contains the idols of preseedings deities) from Kesaram village to Durajpally, during the inverting hours Saturday and Sunday.

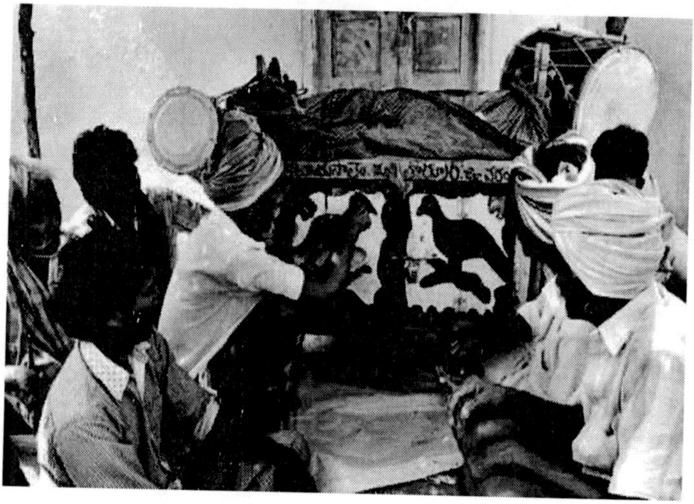

The preseeding deities Sri Lingamanthulu Swamy,believed an incarnation of lord Shiva and his sister Choudamma are offered various poojas during the 5days. Though primarily the yadava community takes part in huge members of peoples from all castes and religions from telanga,Andhra Pradesh, Madhya Pradesh,Maharastra, Odisha,Karnataka, and Tamilnadu people come to the place located just 5km from Suryapet district head quarters. Meanwhile, a huge number of temporary shops have around the hill rock. A day before othe commencement of jathara celebration. On the first Sunday, the women devotees will go round the temple by carrying the "Gampa" it is one of the special event in the Peddagattu Jathara. On the following day devotees will offer bonam to the preseeding deity.

Chandrapatnam

Chandrapatnam ritual will be performed on the third day of jathara, while the priests would velavalm. Ritual on the fourth day, there will be concluding celebrations on the last day of that is the fifth day on Thursday. Here jathara priests all are yadava community people do that everything in this festival. And finally this is the most popular folk festival in the telangana state and neighborings states.

Conclusion

As a study and who practices folk arts, the manner in which jathara takes place and if the customs of the people participating in the jathara are observed, jathara is a folk art show. The folk show their devotion to the art of their worship in front of their deity. Orchestral instruments they play during the horoscope. Like Gajjelu, Dappulu, Doollu, Kommulu, Maps (Rangoli), singing songs,Dances etc., all are the folk art forms. In a sense, without folk art form and exhibition there is no jathara celebration. They do any event during the jathara is associated with the folk art objectives. Before God, playing different types of folk instruments,dancing, singing in folk language, dressing up, laying the pictures during the kalyanam of God, these all are also folk art forms. Folk arts are performed in such context and folk art are still alive.

REFERENCES

1. PSM Laxmi, yaathra vyasaalu.
2. V. Prakash, Telangana movement.
3. Telugu Academy, Telangana charithra, Samskruthi.
4. T. Karunakar Reddy, "Divine box" is taken to the peddagattu jathara, The Hindu.
5. Jayashankar K, Talladillutunna Telangana, Hyderabad Centre for Telangana Study.
6. Nandini sidhareddy, Telangana Soyi.

CHAPTER – 14

Cultural Perspective on Telangana Movement

NEMMADI SAIDULU

Introduction

The Telangana movement took place in two stages. The first phase was the 1969 area. Second phase from 2009 to 2014. The main reason for the success of the second stage movement is to fail the first stage movement. This concept was made for every village and village in the state of Telangana. If we recognize the reason for this, it can be said to everyone in a cultural sense. Especially during the movement, songs in the public have played an important role in the spread of emotion.There are three main reasons for the coming of telangana movement. One is resource exploitation, the second is discrimination (in language, culture, traditions), the third is oppression. There are other reasons, but these are the main ones. Exploitation of resources is looting water from here. Coal is being looted. We wrote such a robbery in the form of songs.After listening to a lecture, the mind sings a song in a tired moment, which gives the power of a tired mind again. There is no doubt that telangana songs have also energized the movement and reached the target. The concept of movement has been spread in everyone as these songs show the injustice of telangana in water, funds and appointments.

Telangana Movement - Song Urgency

Jayashankar's Three Pronged Method

Jayashankar said three methods to transmit the Telangana movement in those days. The movement has to take three steps, he said. First is the conception. So many people are not aware of what is going on in Telangana. Don't know which way exploitation of resources is going on. It is not known how insults are done based on language. It is not known how discrimination continues. All this, the first level of expression must be said. The latter is construction. The place should be built. Organizations need to be formed. Activity should be done. It also needs a political party. The third is also a political magazine. When we publish our ideology and hardship by other magazines, we should publish our ideology and our difficulties in our magazine.

Telangana Movement - Songs Jathara

And how this expression should take place, and there can be some expression through speeches. But it does not reach all sections of society. How then? As emotion joins all groups, it is possible through songs. All groups wanted their minds to be joined by songs. To this end, **the first song was written by Gaddar garu "amma telangaanamaa aakali kekala ganama".** The songs that came out in the first stage had nothing to do with telangana and everything was hungry. How long is the hunger in telangana? Nothing yet? From the point of view, the song of telangana needs something else, and the next generation thinks. In telangana, people sing songs that are difficult and happy. When the famine came, **"vanamma vanamma vanamma okkasaaraina vachipove vaanammo"** and we were singing in the rain god. Also, if the god of rain is merciful and raining with pleasure,**"Naageti saalallo naa telangaanaa naa telangaana"**

At that time, telangana said, if the shell is broken, the shell is going to catch it. He has telangana and culture for answering. Telangana has a grammatical language. In the form of a proper telugu and telangana language is still alive. Telangana culture is great. Telangana customs great to say that telangana language is great, to say the glory of telangana, got my telangana my telangana song in **"Naageti saalallo naa telangaanaa naa telangaanaa"** This is a song that came to us to say that there is somthing in telangana. Telangana people have been supporting the song since August 1997, when it came in August 1997. One of the early movement days, the movement for two songs now reached a high level with uncountable songs. In the early days, there were counted as one and two singers but hundreds of singers came to this malidasa movement. Fewer than five thousand songs. There are at least fifteen hundred to two thousand singers. In the early days, singers asked the writers to turn around and write songs. But for a few days the history of the singers himself sung the songs is seen in the telangana movement.Is the song adorned? Or? Is it language? Isn't it? Does it have a sculpture? Or? Separate this debate. But the song needed for the movement was provided by the singers.

The eloquent person must write the song himself. He must tie himself good. He must sing the song himself. Then he is called the linguist. To this end, all the artists involved in the telangana movement may be eloquent. **Mittapalli surender, jayaraj, goretti venkanna, andeshree and ashok teja are vaggeyakars**. The song for the transmission of emotion played a key role in the telangana movement and sparked the movement.Telangana song is said to have the power to the rest of the song. Where it came from is folk. The folk body reaches the other men and is soft moist. Telangana song has got the power of making the song of the modern trends of folk life. Telangana songs are widely used in localism, language, idioms and nationalities. The simplest language, telangana life, hardship etc., is used. The pallavi selection and moves are great. The song attracts us just as we start. By taking the songs we had in the movement, we were able to give a strong answer to the moves. **Nuv raavachu povachu royyalammukovachu. Nuv idly bandi nadupukovachu nenemi anledu. Viswanaatha, sri sri laku vinamramga mokkutham. Nuv harichandruni padyam paadithe once more kuda vintam kaani cecreteriat lo chakram thipputa matram kudaradu.** Singing this style.The move determines how powerful the move is that the song really has so much power. We have developed ourselves hyderabad. When you did not have anything, **goretti venkanna replied by a song.Annunte unchuko ninnu adigithe chepputho kottu. Emi lenollame mari em peekaneekochinav.**

The song says that this level is necessary to hurt the other person's pride.Hyderabad is ours, **Ayyonivaa nuv avvonivaa telangaanoniki thoti paalonivaa chaarminaaruku sunnamesinava golkondaku rallu mosinavaa** Others have no answer. This motel brought a good sense of humor using the move of the refrainTelangana poets are also in the field of cinema. We all know that **chandala keshavadasu** wrote songs for the first film. But we know that keshavadas was the result of the central telangana movement. He is the khammam district who wrote the song **"“Bale manchi chouka beramu”.**

Dhoom - Dhaam Programmes

One of the songs in telangana come. Songs with chorus come. The songs came in with the band simultaneously. At one stage, telangana songs were not broadcast on andhra channel and there was a risk of banning those channels. So they also aired telangana songs. The game, song and word of the telangana movement are all together. It is not known when and when to sing, when to talk and when to dance. So it transformed into an art form. Dhoom is coming to this order. This telangana dhoom dam was first started by rasamyi balakishan in kamareddy. The second one was in rangareddy and the third was in siddipet. When these bullets came to hyderabad, thousands of volunteers came and played. The dhoom dham program was held on a large scale with telangana artists in hyderabad. In fact, such an event has never happened before. The ease of these instruments is that most instruments do not require. If there is a drum or dappu enough. Telangana people are not impressed by drinking fresh water. He also knows eating biryani. The song can also be accompanied by two or three instruments. If you have the same instrument, you can play with one another. With these songs, there are many audio cassettes. These need to be collected that requires a full range of research. Video cassettes have also come. Until then, as a result of the telangana movement, the telangana songs have reached the level of ringtone. Telangana songs are also made on yo lot of songs have come to show the glory of

telangana. "Nagati salalo na telangana" is a song written by nandini siddhareddi, the songs of "ganama telanganama" written by goreti venkanna are specially songs of telangana glory youtube. A lot of songs have come to show the glory of telangana. **"Nagati salalo na telangana" is a song written by nandini siddhareddi, the songs of "ganama telanganama" written by goreti venkanna** are specially songs of telangana glory.

It is the telangana song that has the power to win dictatorship in the world. Thousands of songs come in any movement, it is in a telangana movement. In the face of globalization, songs on rural destruction have come. **"Etlunnave na palle" "palle kanneeru peduthundo"** "songs come. **Nethala kishore wrote "Etlunnave naa palle".** There are songs on the destruction of the village, **"oyamma na palle endukintha chinnaboye".** The power of a song with two hundred stanzas comes from telangana. Will destruction in the countryside? Nothing else? **Goretti venkanna wrote the song "Naa palle andaalu ".** The black sneeze tree in the countryside is also beautiful.

Pommante povendiraa ori androda, e aapisu metlekkinaa jilledammajitta, this type songs are came. **Mitra** was written the song, **"kaamudilaa mana gudiselu kaali pothe Ramoji middeletla periginaira". Aadudam dappulla daruvaira".** Ramoji increase one acre, 10 acres, and 100 acres are occupied, our huts will be burned down like kamudu.

Awesome Songs on Martyrs

Osmaniya campus lo udayinchina kiranmaa veera telangaanama The song that swung the movement was a familiar song to all of us. At that stage, the song was so exciting that it was a song that had to be written again if it was to be

written again. That song is all about power. A child sings it somewhere in a remote village. Does that child know the osmania campus? Don't know but that is our ray saying. Even a villager was enlightened by the songs he sang. Jai telangana, the child of the seventh grade, the media with him telangana means you know, telangana if you come to telangana, what will happen to you. He answers that my children get jobs. What do you mean by PhD student in the same andhra region? If you ask me, I do not know. If you are together, you will feel comfortable. They have no answer but this. We tell you one reason why we have a hundred reasons to break up.During the movement, kodati wrote a song called asidula harati. Kodati srinu is not known to anyone until then Mitra chlo dhoom dam was written as an art form to sing. **Mathadi dunki aligu pari nattu, chalo dhoom dam telangana jatara vachera**. There is no such thing as telangana songs, which means that there is no other disrespect. Telangana songs have so much variation in telangana life. Not all songs are the same, but we are not listening. There is a variation of the song, the song. **"Raathi bommallona koluvaina shivudaa raktha bandam viluva neeku**

teliyadura" the song sung by the dead srikantachari. Whether the students were fit, they soon got the songs. Telangana students may not be physically present in us in the form of songs they live.

"Amarulaku johaar veerulaku johaar" written by mittapalli surender. During the movement, **a song written by daruvu ellanna was written by veerulara vandanam vidyaarthi amarulaaraa vandanam paadaalaku.** There are six thousand songs in the movement. These songs have made a difference in the life of the people of telangana.

Conclusion

The songs during Telangana movement became very popular in telangana. It is also introduced some new art forms to the world. In my paper to covered introducing singers, writers and artists from all parts of telangana. Introduced new leadership in telangana. Many fluctuations have sustained. The leaders who participated in the hunger strike then breathed and supported them. The song has gained telangana today by crossing such steps. That's why today telangana people are crowned telangana song.

REFERENCES

1. Nandini sidhareddy, Telangana pata 1997, Aavarthanam 2011.
2. Goreti Venkanna, Alasandravanka
3. Prof. Jayashankar, Oduvani muchata
4. Jayashankar K, Talladillutunna Telangana, Hyderabad Centre, Telangana Studies
5. Nandini sidhareddy, Telangana Soyi.

CHAPTER – 15

Role of Dalits in Hyderabad State : A Selected Study

SUREPALLY – UPPALAIAH

Introduction

Hyderabad state was one of the largest princely state in India. Hyderabad state was under the rule of Nizams. In Nizam's state Zagirdars, Jamindars, Deshmukhs and Deshpandes enjoyed powers under the approval of the nizam. They dominated over the weaker sections. People who belonged to downtrodden castes used to perform vetti to Zamindars. Dalits were also used to perform free labour as Begaris, Neeradis, Bhagela by cutting woods and carrying carts. In Hyderabad state many organization such as Aryasamaj and Andhra Mahasabha strived hard against discrimination against dalit. In Hyderabad state, Andhra Mahasabha (started in 1930) took several resolutions against. Untouchability, Vetti. Andhra mahasabha conducted a meetings and published a small booklet on Vetti Chakiri. The Mir Osman Alikhan (VII Nizam of Hyderabad state) brought out a forman against vettichakiri. Dalit leaders in Hyderabad state took a great step about development and mobilization of dalits in Hyderabad.

In Hyderabad state there are many dalit leaders to fight against Nizam rule and mobiliation dalit people to learn

Education and their occupational training and also abolition of social evils among dalits. The famous dalit leaders are Bhagyareddy Varma, B.S. Venkat Rao, Arigeramaswamy, Bathula shyam Sunder etc.

Bhagya Reddy Varma (1888 – 1939)

Bhagya Reddy Varma was born on 1888 May 22 at Hyderabad. His parents names called Madari Venkaiah and Rangamamba. His original name called Madari Bhagaiah. Bhagya Reddy denoting Reddy as 'Redu' the ruler. During his childhood Bhagya Reddy Varma left home and joined Roman catholic brothers tennis court as a Picler boy.

Bhagyareddy Varma joined as an electrical engineer in the Electrical department in 1912. His main aim was upliftment of dalits in all regions. He is efficient in English, Hindi, Marathi, Kannada and Tamil languages. In 1906 he founded **Jagan Mitra Mandali**, the main objective of this mandali to impart education to dalits. He started 'Vaidika Dharma Prachara Sabha' on 1910, this sabha to create awareness among the dalits. Arya samaj gave a title called Varma to Bhagya Reddy Varma ini 1913 for his social service into the Hindu society and dalits. Bhagya Reddy Varama started Swastika volunteer corps on 1912 to give service to the dalits. In 1911 Varma started 'Manya Sangham' this sangham later redesigned it as the Adi Hindi social serveice league. This social service league service to enlighten people. Varma organized Buddha Jayanthi for the first time at Hyderabad, there are many eminent persons attended this Jayanthi called Padmaja Naidu, Adipudi Somanatha Rao etc. He presided over the first, Andhra desa Panchama Conference at Vijayawada on 1917. In this conference Varma stated that dalits were original inhabitants and hence replaced panchama with Adhi-Andhra.

The first conference of 'Manya Sangam' under the presidentship of papanna at Hyderabad. This social service league attracted several caste Hindus of the state and they actively associated with the league. He strongly believed that dalits were not part of Hinduism. He was a pioneer of the Dalit – Self respect movement in Andhra. Bhagyareddy Varma organized a Adi Hindu Sabha under the leadership of Arundatiya leader Subedar Sayanna on 1925. He also organized Matanga Janasabha. This Sabha passed a resolution against Tiquor and toddy consumption.

Jambava Varma seva samithi made efforts to create awareness among Arundhatiyas. At that time Dalit movements brought awareness among Urban dalits and as well as rural areas. Varma gave a call to bring unity among dalits on 1931. He presided over Adi Hindu conference held at Nagpur in 1933. Which Andhra Mahasabha conferences going on Varma attended the meetings and made them to adopted several resolutions to bring reforms in the society. The proposed resolution on Educational facilities and remove untouchability.

Bhagyareddy Varma conducted Adi Hindu gymnastic competitions under the presidentship of Ramamurthy. He encouraged youth, conducted painting, drawing and craft exhibitions at prem theatre Hyderabad. Bhagyareddy Varma participated in the Adi-Hindu conferences and several meetings in Vijayanagaram and Kakinada. On 1937 Bhagyareddy Varma conducted a meeting and requested the government to allocate ten seats to Adi-Hindus. His life is enormous for Adi Hindu movement. Without Varma there is no Adi-Hindu movement in Hyderabad state. His lifelong service gives to Adi – Hindu Society weaker sections and dalits. Bhagyareddy Varma died on 1939 February 18th.

B.S. Venkat Rao (1896 – 1953)

Bathuala Venkatrao was born in Gasmandi on 1896 December 11. His father name was Bathula Sayanna. He wasa another eminent dalit leader in Hyderabad state. He is greatly inspired by Dr. B.R. Ambedkar. He was popularly known as "Rao Saheb". He is popularly known as 'Hyderabad Ambedkar". He studied opto 9th class in English, Urdu Persian, Marathi and Telugu. He worked as a sculptor in pune before joining the public works department of the Nizam's government. The objective of the getting educated dalits, he formed the youth league of Ambedkarites. He joined Nizam government on 1922 as recruitment officer at nizam sagar project. He formed Adi-Dravida sangham on 1922.

For the encouragement of Dalits, he established Adi-Hindu mahasabha on 1927. He established a "Hyderabad state depressed classes association". He constructed a houses and library in the Ghasmandi area now called **Audinagar**. He worked for removal of social evils and bring unity among dalits. Also constructed eighteen temples in Hyderabad for dalits. B.S. Venkatrao contribution to dalits upliftment in Hyderabad was organized by Dr. B.R. Ambedkar who invited him to preside over the Bombay presidency mahar conference in 1936 at Bombay. He started Ambedkar youth league for the development of youth. He elected as secunderabad contonment Board member in 1938 Municipal Elections. In 1943 he nominated "Nizam defence council. In 1946 unanimously elected as "Nizam State Council". He was a education minister at Mir Layak Ali ministry on 1947. He provided an opportunity to dalit students who passed HSC to join in colleges. He prepared the list of eligible dalit children and sent to Nizam government and British India officers and provded opportunities for pursuing their studies in foreign countries.

He led "Hyderabad depressed classes association by merging several small dalit organizations. He died on 1953.

Arige Ramaswamy (1885 – 1973)

He was born at Ramanakola in Ranga Reddy district. He was most famous Dalit leader in Hyderabad state. He is the contemporary of Bhagya Reddy varma. He worked for dalits and fought against social evils and caste descrimination. He did various jobs like office boy, carpenter, and ticket collector at Bollaram Rail road. He believed Brahmasamaj principles. He founded "Suneeta Bala Samajam" at Kummanaguda in secunderabad. Later this organization change into "**Adi-Hindu Jatiyyonnati Sabha** in 1924. He struggle for abolition of Jogini system. He fight against child marriages, animal sacrifices. He propounded Arundhatiya Philosophy. He founded Arundhaliya Mahasabha and created awareness among the dalits. He was also great reformer like Bhagyareddy Varma.

Bathula Shyam Sunder (1908 - 1975)

He was born on 1908 December 21st in Aurangabad district of Hyderabad state. His father name Manikyam employee of railway at Aurangabad. He did his primary and middle school at Aurangabad on 1925 he got B.A. and LLB degree from Osmania University. On 1942 he presided over 'Depressed Classes Mahasabha. He worked as secretary to scheduled castes federation along with B.S. Venkat rao. In 1944 he attended All India Scheduled Caste Federation meeting held at Nagpur. He worked as president of Osmania University graduates association. He played a crucial role in taking dalit issues to Nizam government. He believed that dalits should be together to get political and social freedom. In 1954, he is president of "All India depressed classes association. In the year 1968, he demanded that the Maratwada University renamed as Dr. B.R. Ambedkar University. Scheduled Castes Federation contested general elections in 1952 and won two seats. Republican party of India was started after scheduled caste Federation. Finally he was most popular leader of dalits in Hyderabad state. There are many other leaders fought against social evils like child marriage etc. in Hyderabad state.

Conclusion

Dalit leaders in Hyderabad state actively participated the conferences and meetings and they took resolution against in equality, and social evils in Hyderabad state. Adi Hindu movement created awareness among Dalits to fight for their rights and became forerunner of later Dalit movements. Dalits actively to fight against caste in equality social evils because of Bhagyareddy Varma, Arige Ramaswamy etc. Dalits participated in the liberation struggles against Zamindari systems at various places of Telangana through the awareness of leaders, Arigeramaswamy, Shyam sunder, Bhagyareddy Varma etc. their constant work for dalits to develop the dalits in Hyderabad state.

REFERENCES

1. Ramesan, Freedom struggle in Hyderabad.
2. V.K. Bawa, The last Nizam Life and Times of Mir Osman Alikhan.
3. Razad Ali Khan, 400 years of Hyderabad.
4. Barry pavier, The Telangana Movement.
5. Briggs H.G., The Nizam, His History and his relations with British, London 1861.
6. Rama Krishna Reddy, V. Economic History of Hyderabad state, Warangal Subha 1911-1950, New Delhi – 1987.

7. D.N. Dhanagare, Peasant Movements in India.
8. Bindu D.G., Peoples struggle in Hyderabad, Hyderabad 1948
9. Jawad Razvi, Political awakening in Hyderabad, Visalandhra Publishing house, 1958.